THE HORSWELL DIARY

1997-2005

By

Prunella Dart

THE
HORSWELL DIARY

First published by
Prunella Dart
Horswell House, South Milton, Kingsbridge, Devon

© Prunella Dart 2005

© Illustrations
Len Hubbard and Geoffrey Ireland

British Library of Cataloguing-in-Publication Data
A catalogue entry for this book is available
from the British Library.

10 Digit ISBN 0-9551532-0-4
13 Digit ISBN 978-0-9551532-0-4

Printed and bound in the UK by
Antony Rowe Ltd
Chippenham, Wiltshire SN14 6LH

Contents

————◦◦◦————

CONTENTS

ACKNOWLEDGEMENTS

At the risk of sounding like a gushing starlet at an Oscar ceremony I do have a lot of people to thank for the creation of this book:

Firstly I should like to thank Pat and Robin Macdonald, Editors of the Village Voice magazine for getting me started and for never giving up hope that my copy might one day arrive on time.

I should also like to thank our local artist Len Hubbard for his skill, generosity and kind permission to use his drawings to illustrate this book.

A big thank you also goes to the production and distribution teams of the Village Voice magazine, and to its readers. Without them and their kind words of encouragement the pages of The Horswell Diary would still be blank.

Sincere thanks are also due to Ken Hathaway of the Crowood Press for his excellent advice and to Jean and Derek of Jean Cussons Typesetting for their kindness, patience and support. Thanks also to Rosemary Mackay, because she's special!

This book is for my husband Michael
and for all our family (including feathered and four-legged friends)
for the copy they have inspired

1

I love this quiet time of year

⸺⟨◦◦◦⟩⸺

I love this quiet time of year. After the rush and excesses of Christmas the sudden peace is like a pause, a slow intake of breath before one rushes headlong into the challenges of a new year. It gives one a chance to reflect on past achievements and an opportunity to formulate one's hopes and goals for the year ahead.

I think back to the first time I saw Horswell House. It was love at first sight. Like finding the Sleeping Beauty slumbering in the forest, waiting for the kiss that would awaken her. I saw an elegant, dignified old lady who had been stripped of her pride; all her treasures stolen and her fine proportions camouflaged by ill-conceived alterations. There were bats and rats, mould and decay.

By the time of the auction the property had been stripped completely bare. Fine moulded cornices and skirting boards had been ripped out along with the fireplaces; all plumbing, heating, piping and electric cabling stolen for scrap. Chimney cowls, glass houses, gates, pumps, stone troughs and garden plants were all gone – to people with no respect for her age or beauty.

Because the house had been unattended for so long the garden had disappeared under a wilderness of brambles, providing an undisturbed haven for every type of wildlife: Ravens and buzzards nested in the trees; huge bumble-bees drifted over the wild flowers and weeds; sizeable adders slunk through the bracken whilst their offspring lay coiled in the sunshine. Adult foxes grazed on apples fallen in the orchard while their cubs played tag or snoozed in the long grass. Squirrels were busy everywhere peeling the bark from sycamore trees, and rabbits quickly demolished all the young plants we had brought with us from our previous home.

At night it became the ghostly house of horror films. The air was filled with the shrill sounds of vixen barking, owls screeching and hooting, and badgers fighting, squealing and thundering as they tore through the undergrowth. Low-flying bats raced down the corridors like fighter planes. Strong winds screamed around the chimney pots with the strangled cries of souls in torment. Windows rattled and doors swung eerily closed.

When this Christmas I stood back and looked at the twinkling Christmas trees, the candles and blazing log fires, the house looked so beautiful and content I felt that at last we had given her back her dignity and that all her ghosts were smiling.

Although our efforts to restore the garden and the determined onslaught of our three dogs have frightened some of our original residents away, the number of birds that come to our feeders are a continuing pleasure. Our breakfast room looks out on to the old stable yard, a cobbled courtyard where we feed the birds twice a day.

Our first callers are our four peafowl who honk like grumpy geese if they think we are running late. They sleep in a 300 year old cork tree at night but swoop down and waddle across the lawn in time for breakfast. Peanuts and digestive biscuits are their favourite, along with cheese and leaves. Unless they are really hungry they leave the ordinary birdseed for the little wild birds that arrive next.

Mostly the peafowl are happy to share their food with the sparrows and blue-tits who bravely hop right up close, but occasionally, as a matter of principle, the peacock will take exception and subject an astounded robin or blackbird to a full display of his quite magnificent tail, causing the smaller bird to blink in amazement – but rarely to give ground.

Imran, the larger of the two peacocks has commandeered both the girls, Jemima and Betty, to be his wives, pecking poor Genghis into submission and ensuring that he has the least of the peanuts. Both cocks are looking stunning now, with their vibrant jewel colours and newly grown tails that sweep the floor with feathers of brightest blue, gold and green. The hens too are looking well, although their only colour is around their necks a ruff of iridescent green, turquoise and gold. After they leave the arena the hanging feeders become alive with little birds. Blackbirds, thrushes, robins, hedge-sparrows, blue-tits, greenfinches, chaffinches, greater and lesser-spotted woodpeckers, collared doves, predatory magpies and screeching jays all take their turn.

This morning they were joined by three fluffy grey squirrels and to my amazement and much honking from the curious peafowl, by a three-legged black-and-white cat who appeared from under the granary! The poor cat was so desperate for food that it ran into the house as soon as I opened the door. It gulped down a saucer of warm milk while our three dogs watched in disbelief, hanging over the half-door between their room and the kitchen. A plate of meat later and another bowl of milk and our surprise visitor disappeared back under the granary where I hope he or she will be safe for the night.

Phone calls to the police have proved unfruitful. I had hoped, with such distinctive markings, we would soon find its owner. It has clearly been a magnificent cat but it is now very, very thin and hungry and its coat matted and dirty and in need of care.

I hope I'll see it again tomorrow. I've saved it some Christmas ham.

After the birds we usually have the fish to feed but now it is too cold. The trout swim slowly in the depths of their pond and do not want to come to the surface, and the goldfish in the fountain are encased in the most amazing ice sculpture, much to the bemusement of a passing heron who flapped away unfed.

The fountain finally trickled to a stop forming spectacular icicles and sculpted curves. The cherub in the centre now looks as though he's holding a crystal ball aloft in the palm of his hand.

With a new year just beginning it looks not only beautiful, but prophetic and surreal.

MARCH 1997

The passage of Hale-Bopp...

—◦◦◦—

The passage of Hale-Bopp through our heavens has coincided with a period of such intense change and activity that I too have felt I was a traveller through time and space. It has been an extraordinary few weeks in which people, places, and cultures have tumbled and swirled together like brilliant beads in a kaleidoscope, forming first one pattern and then another to delight and amaze the eye.

It began in Thailand where, with my mother to celebrate her 70th birthday, we strolled along silver sands and swam in warm turquoise seas. The greyness of an English winter was lost in a riot of tropical colour, lush vegetation and the warm smiles of a gentle nation. Talking with my sister, who joined us from New Zealand, I was reminded of my colonial roots and of gloriously carefree days together travelling to one South Sea island after another, living off rice and fish, and gazing up at the stars through the gaps in the palm thatch.

Back in London, having exchanged bare feet and a sarong for an evening dress and pearls, I accompanied my husband to his Livery Company dinner held in the Barber Surgeons' Hall.

The ancient traditions and essential Englishness of the evening's ceremony chased sweet memories of Thailand from my head like butterflies in the wind; Asian smiles replaced by British sang froid.

Home to Horswell and our menagerie, now extended to include ornamental ducks on the pond. Horatio and Sir Francis, the two new Carolina drakes, stand on an overhanging branch looking, with their 'fore and aft' hats, like admirals on the bridge surveying their fleet. Dogs rush to greet us and peacocks screech their welcome. The answering machine is laden with messages from people who want to come and stay, or who are already 'en route', and the garden screams for our attention.

We roll up our sleeves and throw ourselves into a maelstrom of cooking, cleaning, gardening and laundry, entertaining visitors from all corners of the earth, so numerous and continuous that their names and faces stream from memory like the tail of the comet, their passing marked most noticeably by the increasing mountain of sheets and table napkins waiting to be laundered. Shrouds discarded by departed ghosts.

We escape to Egypt and a dream come true: A time warp. We cruised from Luxor to the Aswan Dam. Our ship became our time-machine, carrying us from the wonders of man three thousand years ago to the advanced technology of the twentieth century. We grew to know and recognise gods and goddesses, pharaohs and queens from their cartouches and images carved in the ancient stone of magnificent temples, their lives portrayed in such visual splendour one could feel them live and breathe, mingling in the crowd around us, whispering of love and battles won or lost.

Returning to Britain and reality, my New Zealand passport precludes me from passing through Customs with my husband. Instead I join the queue marked 'Aliens', and contemplate waving my tentacles and oozing green slime. However, I find the inconvenience preferable to exchanging my smart navy passport for a nasty red one which closely resembles an edited edition of 'The Thoughts of Chairman Mao'.

Although not keen to become one, I do like Europeans, especially one particular family of French people. Which is fortunate because they came to stay within days of our return, replacing thoughts of ancient Egypt with those of croissants and Carte Noire coffee. Whilst I tried to dissuade

Mme Normand from cooking the snails she had collected from the garden, (which she assured me would be delicious with a little parsley and garlic butter), my husband found an urgent need to visit the farm, family and friends in Oxfordshire. The duration of his stay? One English-speaking week.

My French-speaking week was exhausting – but amusing too. Especially when my guests offered to deadhead all the daffodils in the orchard. Cutting off noble heads seemed such a peculiarly French thing to do. I felt like getting out my knitting and whistling the Marseillaise... except I can't knit or whistle. Another reason for not being European perhaps.

A 5.00 a.m. start to take them to their ferry meant the possibility of having a much-needed day to ourselves. Returning from Plymouth my heart lifted to see my husband waiting on the front doorstep to greet me but was quickly dashed when, finger to his lips, he whispered that we had three unexpected guests waiting upstairs.

Appalled, I fixed a smile on my face and followed him reluctantly up the front stairs. There, on the landing, I was greeted by a sight bizarre beyond belief. Stretched out contentedly on the beige carpet, were our three visitors... Imran, Genghis and Jemima, three of our peafowl, their beautiful feathers gleaming in the sunshine that streamed through the window. They seemed quite surprised to be asked to leave but slowly got up, one by one, and walked elegantly down the stairs, their tails rustling like taffeta ballgowns behind them, along the stone corridor, across the kitchen and out through the door to the courtyard – through which they had entered – thankfully leaving no mess behind them.

Perfect guests in fact.

3

May 1997

The last time I saw Jane

———◈◈◈———

The last time I saw Jane was over a cold bottle of Chablis in a smart new restaurant near her London Office.

She had just been promoted to a fantastic job in publishing and I had successfully launched a new design business. We had a lot to celebrate and, not having seen each other for many, many years, a lot of reminiscing to do. We've known each other forever and the conversation soon veered off marketing strategies and circulation numbers towards the finer points of newt catching and my dismal attempts to vault over the wooden horse in the school gym which, maddeningly, she still seemed to find screamingly funny. Pink with laughter and the effects of the Chablis we finally headed back to our respective business meetings, promising that we would get together more often as it had been such fun.

Well, that was twelve years ago, and when last week Jane 'phoned on her way back to London from Cornwall – asking if she could call in on her way by – I suddenly felt wrong-footed and unprepared. Would she think I had opted out, settling for the bucolic country life? Had I let myself go, lost my cutting edge, my city chic? Well, yes, I probably had. But did that bother me? That's what I wasn't sure about.

It had been a hectic month, racing up and down to London, juggling house-sitters and dog-sitters, business and pleasure, balancing family and friends with commitments and chores. Even with the lighter evenings the days are still too short to accommodate all that needs doing, and despite running at full tilt a backlog of work continues to grow. I dream about time warps, expanding time, stretching it so that I can achieve all that I want to do. I wonder if I had a clone if it would halve my workload or double it. I long for the day with nothing prearranged scrawled in haste on the calendar, the luxury of thinking 'What shall I do to-day', the uncertainty of not knowing. To my amazement a friend tells me that she is going to start a part-time job because she has too much time on her hands. I suggest she gives seminars for people like me, revealing the secrets of her success – except that people like me would not have time to attend them.

Some events though I wouldn't miss for the world – well, not intentionally. Like the banquet at the Skinners Hall at which my husband was presented with an award by the Lord Mayor of London. Laden with overnight bags, ballgown and my husband's white tie and tails, rushing against the clock to compensate for the delay on the train, and squeezed into an inadequately-lit lift it was hard not to feel a little rising frustration when the door failed to open at any of the six floors of the hotel. The situation was not eased when my cries for help were answered by an uppity head waiter who sauntered by with a tray of drinks borne high on his shoulder. 'Calm down, Madam', he spat as he swept past, never to return. Needless to say, his comment had exactly the reverse effect.

Two or three others paused briefly to peer at me as one might a captive tiger in a cage before continuing past. Eventually a housekeeper of indeterminate foreign nationality took pity on me and fiddled with the locking mechanism muttering incantations under her breath. Finally with a screech that could have been Swahili for 'Open Sesame', the lock sprang open and I made a dash for freedom, bolting along the corridor to our room for a hasty bath and change of clothes.

An anxious husband awaited me, delighted to be reunited with his suit, albeit at the eleventh hour. Not daring to take the lift we raced down six flights of stairs and fell into the nearest taxi.

'I know you', said the taxi driver.

'Oh?' said my husband. ('Aargh!' thought I.)

'I've carried you before'.

And indeed he had. We must have been his best paying fare of all time. On that occasion we were on our way home, catching the train at Paddington, and had stopped in Saville Row to pick up a suit which had been altered. Being rush hour and taxis in short supply we decided to hold on to our cab whilst my husband popped in to collect the suit. A two-minute operation one might think? Alas, no. Having been regaled with the driver's life history, his aspirations for the future, his theories on life, the planet and the universe for what seemed the best part of an hour, I was relieved to see my husband emerge with his suit albeit to face a cab fare of titanic proportions.

'I've been to Florida since I last saw you!' We nodded dumbly, conscious of our contribution to his travel costs. 'How was the suit?' he asked.

'Expensive!' we chimed in unison.

Another dash to London later in the month was to celebrate a friend's birthday with a Tea Dance at the Waldorf hotel. It was a glittering affair – champagne, chandeliers, marble dance floors, and a Palm Court orchestra. The only think lacking was expertise on the dance floor. Most of us were of an era when ballroom dancing was not considered an essential social grace. We could all remember the Twist, the Mashed Potato and the Hippy Hippy Shake, but were sadly unable to execute a Foxtrot or a Tango or tell the difference between a Quickstep and a Waltz without counting one, two, three, one, two, three under our breath. How I wish I had toughed it out at Miss Murray's School of Ballroom Dancing all those years ago instead of sloping off to join friends for an illicit cigarette at the Juke Box Café. It would have spared me my blushes when on leaving the dance floor fellow partygoers held up two menu cards revealing a damning score of 'Null Points'!

On arrival back home all three dogs rushed unexpectedly out of the front door to greet us. It should have prepared us for the scene awaiting us inside. An empty biscuit tin and a house strewn with dogs' hairs bore testament to a life of total indulgence in our absence. No wonder Bertie covers his head with his paws and mopes for hours when the dog-sitter goes home.

The garden is rapidly coming alive with the mild weather and ducks and birds seem to think spring has arrived. The peacocks have started displaying their beautiful tails and calling to one another from the tree-tops and our pair of mallards flew past the bedroom window in a victory fly past to announce the laying of their first batch of eggs. A pair of wild mallards has started to visit our pond and we hope they won't lead our 'tame' ducks away once the mating season is over. We feed them corn every day to supplement their diet although most of it seems to be eaten by a family of grey squirrels. At least, I suppose if they're stealing the corn they are not stripping the bark from the trees which they would normally do.

The snowdrops were heavenly this year, spreading like snowdrifts under the trees. Now they are beginning to fade, giving way to primroses and a golden sea of daffodils. Maddeningly, a combination of strong winds and rabbit-chasing dogs means that many of the blooms are knocked to the ground. We collect these each day to bring into the house. We call it Bertie's Bouquet since he is the greatest culprit!

My girlfriend Jane seemed smaller when she arrived than I had remembered. But perhaps it was just in contrast to the large powerful car she was driving. Immaculately groomed and full of energy, she told us about her imminent transfer to Cairo, from where she would be commuting on a weekly basis to Moscow to set up the infrastructure of a vast new business enterprise. She talked about her husband, her child, her famous colleagues, of deals done in smart restaurants, and holidays in exotic locations. I thought of the hydrangeas still to prune and the herbaceous border that was crying out for my attention. The prospect seemed suddenly very dull

Later that day I took the dogs for a walk along the cliff path to Bantham. It was a glorious evening. The sky was streaked pink and grey and dark waves were tipped with gold from the setting sun. Flossie and Bertie ran ahead, the wind ruffling their fur. Abo, my loyal old friend, stayed close, plodding along beside me. I thought about Jane's visit. As we walked down the last slope towards Bantham Beach we could see a small figure walking slowly up towards us. It was my husband coming to meet me. The dogs raced forward jumping for joy when they realised who it was. I ran down to join them just as the sun slipped down below the horizon leaving a golden glow in the sky where it had been.

Cairo and Moscow suddenly seemed very unimportant.

4

JULY 1997

The era of a New Dawn?

———◦◦◦———

A consignment of plants ordered in the spring arrived unexpectedly, necessitating a massive clearing, weeding, digging and planting operation under monsoon conditions. Three saturated dogs lay on the cobbles watching us, looking as dejected as only a dog can look. Bedraggled peafowl with rain-flattened feathers peered down from the trees above us, hunched up like grumpy vultures.

We worked all day in rivers of mud, planting in what could have been a paddy field. At 10 o'clock at night we finished. Drenched to the skin and smothered in red earth we staggered wearily back to the house like a couple of Glastonbury revellers, Imran and Genghis screeching approval from their treetop roost.

It's certainly been a very wet month. The ravages of wind and rain have wreaked havoc on our garden flowers. Roses in particular have suffered. They were looking so beautiful but now many have rotted on the stem in full bud, and others have succumbed to the wretched black spot, testimony to our infrequent spraying.

Curiously, though, a pale blush pink rose called *New Dawn* continues to flourish, draping its profusion of blooms gracefully over the courtyard wall. Perhaps it is in tune with the age; 'the New Dawn' seems to be an expression much-used by politicians these days. The Labour party assured us we would enter the 'New Dawn' if we elected them to power. We did, and it has rained ever since. At the hand-over of Hong Kong it rained too, the downpour beating the retreat on HRH The Prince of Wales's naval cap, and washing a tear from the Governor's eye. The Chinese officials there also spoke of a 'New Dawn'. It will be interesting to see if the policies of these new governments remain as pale pink as our rose.

Despite much posturing and dramatic flamenco footwork on the part of our peacocks, the peahens have either failed to be impressed or failed to raise their brood as no chicks have been seen. We suspect the crows may have taken their eggs. The ducks too gradually lost their brood:

After a lengthy sit on a great pile of eggs the Carolina duck was seen proudly swimming across the pond followed by a line of little dark duck-lings no bigger than a bumble bee. We have been feeding the trout in the pond for four years now, and although numbers of trout have decreased those that remain are very large indeed. Sadly, we think they may have been responsible for taking the ducklings as, within minutes, one by one they disappeared. We were shocked by their loss. The suddenness of their death makes one reflect on how very precious and fragile the gift of life is. It's something we take for granted, even moan about at times, and yet in a trice it can be taken from us.

I was reminded of this again later in the month when we were in London for our youngest grand-daughter's christening in Lincoln's Inn Chapel. Sunlight shafted through richly stained glass into the dark somnolent chapel. Unusually quiet young cousins looked on with eager expectant faces whilst little Olivia, a beautiful baby with big blue eyes and rosebud lips, blinked away water poured over her head from a shell. Perfect. Safe. Surrounded by love, by family and friends. I thought of our ducklings and all the other babies equally innocent, trusting and vulner-able beyond the sanctuary of those ancient hallowed walls. That anything so pure, so perfect, could ever be unloved, starved, neglected, abused or violated seemed unbearably shocking.

And yet one reads every day in the news of such terrible crimes against society, against nature and against life itself. It is a conundrum that only experience of life can teach one to truly value it. Thus the dawn of realisation can often come too late to be effective:

I read in the paper that the recent landing of Pathfinder on Mars 'ushers in a new era of exploring Earth's neighbours for traces of water and perhaps life'. I sense that having trashed one planet we are looking for another. But wait a minute. With its dry rocky landscape, polluted dust and poisonous 95% carbon dioxide atmosphere doesn't it all sound a little familiar? Holes in the ozone layer? Increased radiation? Deforestation? Water shortages? Toxic waste? Exhaust emissions? ... Are we sure we haven't lived there before?

Perhaps leaving Mars was civilisation's first step towards a better life – and it was the colonisation of Earth that was meant to be the real New Dawn?

5

SEPTEMBER 1997

Look thy last on all things lovely…

———◦◦◦———

For a few stormy days it looked as if summer was over and autumn had arrived. But then, just as I was resigning myself to long dark afternoons making chutney, the sunshine returned and I was granted a reprieve. The dogs and I could resume our daily swims at the beach.

The word 'beach' is on a par with the word 'dinner' in the canine rapid-response stakes. A mere whisper of it will send all three dogs into a barking frenzy and a headlong dash to the back of the car, for in the words of John Masefield:

'…the call of the running tide is a wild call and a clear call that may not be denied'.

Flossie, the young border collie, adores the water and is a fearless swimmer. In fact her coat has become so thin this summer I wonder if she's turning into a fish. Abo, our faithful black Labrador, who on land is plagued with arthritis, becomes as sleek as an otter in the water, disappearing under the surf to pick up a stick or a stone, undaunted by the waves breaking around him.

Meanwhile, big hairy Bertie, who is the Joker in our pack, immerses himself until completely sodden and then sits on my clothes, on the beach, keeping guard.

One morning we were joined by a small school of dolphins breaching and tail-flapping as they passed westwards along the coast. A wondrous reminder that we really do live in paradise here in the South Hams.

It seems that Horswell too has its own special enchantment. So many of our summer visitors have been touched by their stay with us that some have said they fear they will never find us again – that it was all a dream, a mirage.

Others have been found lingering in the bedrooms, not wishing to leave. All of them have said that they feel refreshed and revitalised. Perhaps the spirit of the old Horse Well – where travellers stopped and watered their horses and rested a while – lives on. I like to think so.

Despite the sunshine, signs of autumn are all around us. Spiders are spinning their horizontal webs across the grass, the first mushrooms have appeared, and congregations of rooks and crows quarrel in the treetops after a hard day gleaning the barley stubbles. A pair of buzzards hover on the rising air and kestrels wheel and swoop, calling out to each other with their high-pitched 'Mew, mew'. The ducks are coming out of their moult, once more acquiring their distinctive markings but the peacocks, now having shed their magnificent long tail feathers, are looking a little unbalanced and self-conscious.

Imran has commandeered both wives and, as I write, all three of them are snuggled down on the gravel beside me, their eyes closing drowsily in the sunshine. Under the new pecking-order Genghis now feeds alone, often from our hands, and for company snoozes on the window ledge to be near us.

The cooler nights have reduced the number of bats, thank goodness. No more blood-chilling squeals from guests sleeping in the four-poster bed as they see a little piggy face peering upside down from the canopy! Or having to duck as they swoop like low-flying jets along the corridors. The double whammy of horrors is to be in the cellar, and encounter a bat and step on a toad simultaneously. My husband is finding it effective protection for his wine stocks. I am even beginning to wonder if these bats are radio-controlled, as they seem particularly evident when his mother-in law comes to stay.

The big-game season has also begun. Alerted by my screams, my intrepid husband, armed only with his '*Little Nipper, world-patented and spring-loaded mousetrap*' has been making courageous forays into the hinterland of my pantry in fearless pursuit of a band of marauding mice which seem the size of small kangaroos. Too squeamish to do my own trapping, I offer encouragement through the door, telling him that in this age of female equality a little machismo is a good thing. I only hope we don't have to mount his trophies on the study wall.

The garden, too, senses the pressure is off, the summer ending. The lawn is losing its stripes; the flower borders beginning to fade and droop leaving the Michaelmas daisies to carry the flag. Box-hedging is growing out of shape and the wisteria, long overdue to be pruned, takes advantage of our absence to strangle jealously a nearby rose. Nature is flexing its muscles for a takeover.

We must get to work and yet the sad events of the last week have left us devastated and devoid of energy. Before her tragic and untimely death, Diana, Princess of Wales, had said that she saw her role as that of a messenger. Perhaps the greatest message of her sudden death is that we, who take so much for granted, should value life.

I like the words of Walter de la Mare:

> '*Look thy last on all things lovely,*
> *Every hour – let no night*
> *Seal thy sense in deathly slumber*
> *Till to delight*
> *Thou has paid thy utmost blessing*'

6

CHRISTMAS 1997

The trial of the English nanny

———◦◉◦———

The trial of the English nanny accused of murdering a young American baby in her care has made me think how society becomes desensitised by an over-exposure to horrific events. How, after a while, one fails to react in a normal way and begins to accept what is horrible as the norm. It is only when death occurs that we seem to register real shock, stop in our tracks and re-evaluate a situation.

This awareness was reinforced by the controversial *Sensation* exhibition at the Royal Academy. The exhibits, often shocking, present familiar objects in unfamiliar ways, extending one's perceptions, activating thoughts and altering perspectives. But above all, jolting the viewer from his apathetic acceptance of the status quo. The fact that it takes an image as provocative as a dead sheep in a tank or a picture of Myra Hindley to do that is a harsh statement of the times in which we live and the level of normality which we now accept.

Returning from London on the train, I felt my heart lift the nearer we got to home. That part of the journey from Exeter St. David to Newton Abbot, beside the water, via Exmouth and Dawlish Warren, must surely be one of the most scenic bits of railway in England. I love the intellect, the culture, the variety and the pace of city life but the taste of the salt in the air as I arrive home is like nectar and the greeting of husband and dogs sheer heaven.

It's hard to believe that Christmas is just around the corner when only yesterday the dogs and I were at the beach, swimming in the sea and making the most of the November sunshine. At the farm in Oxfordshire hard frosts have already turned the trees and the hedgerows wonderful rich autumn colours. Spindleberries and wild cherry leaves stand out red against rusty oaks and golden beech, whilst here our milder climate allows summer to linger on with roses and geraniums still in flower and trees still quite heavy with leaves. Only the chill wind and the long dark evenings remind us that winter is on its way.

The dogs, too, sense the changing seasons and creep in to lie beside the Aga after a hard day's squirrel-chasing. Except Bertie that is. Bertie sees ghosts in the kitchen and suddenly scoots off to hide under the long tablecloth in the breakfast room, eventually peering out with wide frightened eyes like a big black wolf in Red Riding Hood's bonnet.

We're not too sure whether Bertie actually knows he is a dog. Since we took him in as a stray he's grown into the most extraordinarily independent character with a distinct mind of his own. We sometimes think he might be the reincarnation of a previous owner of Horswell and that he regards us, somewhat disdainfully, as his personal cook and butler.

He has spent so much time in the office recently that we call him the Secretary. He even has his mail sent here now, or so we assume from the number of letters we receive addressed: To the Secretary, Horswell House. He seems to be working to a secret agenda, sloping off to the office chair as soon as our backs are turned... and feigning sleep whenever we discover him. A particularly high telephone bill coincided with the recent plunge in the stock market and we're beginning to suspect Bertie of some covert share dealing. Certainly I found him with my Times portfolio card clenched between his teeth and the business pages in shreds all over the floor after a particularly rough day's trading.

My mother returns from America this week, where she's been staying with her sister and cousins various. The Oregon connection are a wild bunch. The men are big, salmon-fishing, elk-hunting sort of men.

Men with fists of steel and hearts of gold. The women are small and feisty, women for whom 'going shopping' means making a visit to the hardware store. Aunt Margaret at 75 and 5'2" drives a red Jeep, carries a Smith & Wesson.38, plays a mean game of poker and rules them all with an iron will. Their warmth, generosity, and spending power, are legendary. I call them the Hole in the Wall Gang, with Aunt Margaret as the cashpoint queen.

A rather shy girlfriend is collecting my mother from Heathrow for me. She's worried she may miss her. I haven't dared tell her that it's highly unlikely: Last time she returned draped in an Indian blanket, wearing a Stetson and with a vast set of moose antlers mounted on her trolley!

Thankfully she will be home in time for Christmas as the selection and decoration of our Christmas tree is an annual ritual that we all enjoy. The trees have to be very large. Ideally, big enough to wedge unsupported between ceiling and floor. Vast quantities of boxes are brought up from the cellar and there's lots of excitement as old favourites and forgotten treasures are unwrapped from their tissue-paper. My girlfriend and I then run up and down step ladders placing decorations whilst my mother, fortified with sherry and mincepies, gives stage directions from a suitably positioned armchair. We normally do two trees – one silver, gold and twinkly, the other red, green and traditional. It takes us forever and I'm never sure if the resulting weariness is from the effort, the chatter, the sherry or the childlike enthusiasm. I suspect the latter. I love Christmas. From midnight mass to the last pine needle it all goes by far too quickly.

I hope you too will have a very happy Christmas with special moments to treasure, and can look forward to a bright new year.

7

JANUARY 1998

A bad bout of the Millennium Blues

———◆◆◆———

I have been waiting for my usual New Year optimism to inspire my pen, but it's no good. I have a bad bout of the Millennium Blues.

Of course, it could be just the aftermath of a hectic and over indulgent Christmas. That low, exhausted feeling when the decorations are packed away in boxes for another year, all the guests have gone home and the house looks empty and bare.

But memories of fun and laughter linger on, like the look of boyish delight when my husband discovered a train set amongst his presents. Carriages and track were quickly assembled and soon the Calgary Express was choo choo chooing its way around the Dining Room table, complete with American sound effects, realistic chuffing noises and smoke trailing from a gleaming smokestack. It delayed Lunch so long we did think of adapting it to carry the vegetable dishes but thought the repetitive 'Whoo Whoo', 'Clang Clang' and 'All aboard' might prove a little too distracting.

Eventually it was shunted off into a siding, enabling us to eat Lunch, (which had now become Dinner), watched by two attentive peafowl huddled on the windowsill. Fortunately, by this stage, the turkey was so overcooked that it no longer sufficiently resembled a bird to give them any cause for alarm.

Maybe it's the weather that's making me anxious? The sight of our poor tormented trees thrashing helplessly in the gales. The incessant wind that snatches at my clothes and tangles my hair. The whine and roar of the storm as it screams through the woods uprooting oak trees and tearing branches limb by limb from mighty pines. The thud as it slams against the house, rattling shutters and scattering slates. The lawns strewn with twigs and debris, the gardens bleak and saturated. Thunder cracks and lightening flashes. Surely one could be forgiven for wondering if 'The End of the World', is indeed, 'Almost Nigh'?

But whilst I fret and feel like joining Bertie under the tablecloth, Flossie the sheepdog runs for joy, energised by the storm and loving the feel of the wind in her fur. Meanwhile Abo our Labrador, a natural opportunist, sneaks off in search of dustbins bowled over by the wind, or maybe a bitch whose scent has been blown his way.

Although he can disappear at the speed of light, his arthritis eventually slows him up and his homeward journey is a pathetic sight which he plays to full effect in the hope of attracting a lift. Despite his vile smell and muddy undercarriage his success rate is quite high and we are immensely grateful to the many people who have brought him home, as, surprisingly really, we do adore him. At first it was a kindly neighbour who used to stop for him. He was so relieved to see her that he promptly fell asleep, snoring, on the back seat of her car and had to be woken on arrival. Then it was a girlfriend in a smart red Porsche who fell for his charms, despite his agricultural odour, but the pinnacle of his success was being chauffeured home in an immaculate powder blue Mercedes. He arrived triumphantly, perched, nose in air, on the front passenger seat whilst the owner's elegant wife and her more pleasantly perfumed pooch were relegated to the back. Since then his forays have become less frequent and we're doing our utmost to get him to quit whilst he's ahead.

So it's an ill wind that blows no good. The ducks are enjoying the muddy puddles where the pond has overflowed, the wild birds swing in the wind like metronomes as they cling to the peanut feeders and even the peacocks have put thoughts of Spring on hold, enabling them to share the same territory and huddle together for shelter. Even a mink seen stealing away from the trout pond escaped reprisals, the wind making him too quick (or too politically correct!) to become a fur collar.

It it's not the weather, perhaps it's the Millennium Dome that's adding to my apocalyptic malaise. Apparently it's going to be divided into eleven zones, each showcasing different aspects of man's life on earth today and in relation to the universe. E.g. Body, Mind, Soul, Work, Rest, Play etc: A monument to the achievements, technology, lifestyle and spirituality of society today.

A few thousand years ago a King called Cheops built the Great Pyramid in Egypt, exemplifying the most advanced technology of its age. Recently, historians and mathematicians have discovered that its whole construction, with its labyrinth of passages and chambers is rich with information about the universe; that every dimension is relevant, containing the key to pure mathematics. It represents an archive of hidden knowledge that if read correctly speaks intelligibly, intellectually and religiously to all people and is 'a testimony to the wisdom and technology of a lost civilization'.

With my current 'Fin de Siecle' fatalism I'm wondering if Mr. Mandelson is going to be the Cheops of the 21st Century, and if the Millennium Dome is also 'a testimony to a lost civilization'. Another cryptic wonder of the world to be unearthed by future generations when all traces of life as we know it have disappeared.

I'm sure that when the wind stops and the sun comes out my usual happy mood will return, but, in the meantime, if you see me lashing fallen branches together to form a raft, and forming our livestock into rows two by two, don't be surprised.

8

May 1998

'A gentleness in hearts at peace'...

———◦◦◦———

Two weeks ago I was wondering if my geraniums would survive their sprinkling of snow. To-day it is so hot that the dogs are lying in the shade under the Jeep whilst Genghis, our lonesome peacock, is stretched out on its roof, soaking up the sunshine. He and Imran had their annual cockfight yesterday to determine territory and ownership of the two hens for the forthcoming mating season. They flew at each other with their spurs extended, screeching and pecking ferociously and trampling on one another's magnificent tails. Poor old Genghis didn't seem to put up much of a fight this year, quickly bowing to his inevitable defeat. Meanwhile Imran, his feathers puffed up and tail fully displayed, strutted around the courtyard with the precise steps and arrogance of a flamenco dancer, his head thrown back crowing victory to the far hills with a raucous screech.

Jemima and Betty seem resigned to the outcome and, now that the battle is over, are snoozing in the cool earthy scrapes they have dug in the rose bed. Above them, perched triumphantly on the stone ball at the top of a tall gatepost, Imran preens himself in the sunshine, his chest and head the colour of burnished lapis lazuli, the green and golden feathers of his long sweeping tail shimmering like silken threads in the breeze.

The daffodils are over now, their untidy leaves enabling grass and weeds to grow around them, safe from the mower for some time yet. I shall miss being able to bring armfuls of 'Cheerfulness' indoors, their sweet perfume scenting the whole house. There are still the gentle primroses, cowslips and bluebells to remind us of Spring but already the hot pinks, purples and yellows of the azaleas and rhododendrons hint at Summer, looking almost tropical against the cloudless blue sky.

In the woods the dark skeletal shapes of beech and oak are gradually softening in a haze of palest green as 'the folded leaf is wooed from the bud with winds upon the branch' and, in the orchard, blossoms of pear and apple are scattered like confetti over the trees.

The air is filled with the sound of birdsong, an endless chatter and chirrup and flutter of activity as blackbirds and blue tits, goldfinch and greenfinch, great tit and thrush go busily about their daily tasks. The only other sounds are the rattle of the Sunday papers, the splash of the fountain and the sound of the sea sighing through the trees. In Tennyson's words, '*There is sweet music here that softer falls than petals from blown roses on the grass*' Heaven is having the time to stop and listen to it.

Even paradise has its sadness. Last week three of our ornamental ducks disappeared in a trail of feathers leading to the woods. Two Carolinas with their 'fore and aft' Admiral's hats and our handsome red crested Pochard must have made a tasty dish for a hungry fox, or from the droppings left, perhaps a badger. It seems a cowardly act. The ducks are all so tame they feed from our hands, waddling across the lawn to wait for their food, unafraid of dogs or peacocks. Their death would have been poor sport, particularly as the hens were sitting on eggs, keeping their mates close to home. We are anxious for the remaining female Pochard who is still sitting on her nest, the last male Carolina who has taken over the role of her chaperone and our pair of Mallards whose bright intelligent eyes regard us with such total trust.

In London last month we were invited on an official visit to the Surrey Docks Farm project which is an inner City 'farm' on just 2 acres of land in Bermondsey to initiate underprivileged city children into rural life. Looking at the high rise blocks and treeless streets all around, it is easy to understand that the beauty of the countryside which we can sometimes take for granted, is something the local children would find hard to comprehend. The farm provides a colourful oasis, an escape to another world, a safe haven for the maladjusted, a refuge for children who have been abused and a stimulus to those with learning or emotional problems. The energy, enthusiasm and creativity that emanates from those young people involved in maintaining its existence and running the educational programme was an inspiration, and the power of a few ducks, sheep, goats and chickens to heal the wounds of harsh urban life, was a delight to see.

It reminded me how, as a child, I had immersed myself in the world of Doctor Doolittle, daydreaming of his travels and conversations with his motley crew of animals, safe in their world, far removed from the insecurities of adult life. It's strange how daydreams come true. Sitting here in the sunshine with our dogs and birds around us, the trout in the pond, the fish in the fountain, the old fat toad trying to hide under a leaf and the bumble bee circling my head there is a sense of harmony and mutual understanding of which Dr. Doolittle would have approved. A *'gentleness in hearts at peace under an English Heaven'*.

All I need now to complete the scene is a Pushmepullyou!

9

'More and more beautiful things'...

———◦◦◦———

The last few weeks have passed at breakneck speed, with Horswell entrusted to family and friends, house-sitters and dog-sitters, whilst we try and squeeze a whole summer season into a month, cope with an endless stream of visitors, maintain some semblance of order in the garden, and daydream about catching up on our sleep.

France at least was sunny, not oppressed by the Stygian gloom of overcast skies as we have been. As a country it seems to have flourished in recent years. It appears prosperous and full of vitality. The pace of life, if possible, seemed even quicker than here. Certainly the traffic moves faster.

Swirling round the Etoile in Paris, ten cars deep in rush-hour traffic, I noticed one of my American passengers had disappeared. I had last seen her only seconds before, when a large Citroen estate, seemingly determined to make headway through the side of our car, stopped just a Gitane paper away from certain impact. But then, distracted by the tour bus bearing down on our right flank and accelerating hard to squeeze into a momentarily open gap, I lost sight of her. Edging an incredibly pushy

27

Peugeot off my left bumper and breathing in to avoid the car on my right, I worked my way through a hundred potential collisions to the Champs Elysees. There I resumed my role of Tour Guide and, in an attempt to encourage my passengers to abandon the crash positions they had assumed and enjoy the view, continued my discourse on the various sites that we passed. I was answered by weak groans from under the trembling coat in the footwell beside me. Not until we'd circumnavigated the city twice in an attempt to find our exit from the Peripherique, an operation which brought my map reader (map upside down. 'Sorry, I've dropped my glasses. What was that name again?') perilously close to being dumped off in the Place de la Guillotine, did my missing companion re-emerge, pale and wide-eyed from under her coat to utter the words 'Just wait 'til I tell the folks back home!' What would she tell? That I'd driven five hundred miles to show them Paris – or that she had found two sweet papers and an old Barclaycard receipt under the mat? We bought postcards so that she would know where she had been.

Fortunately the rest of our brief stay in France was less stressful. Lunch with friends in the Loire Valley was a full day event with so many courses and different wines one wondered if there would ever be an end to their generous hospitality. I was reminded how, as a girl, when I had stayed at their farm, on Sundays the whole family would travel from miles around, on foot, in cars, on bicycles and tractors, all bringing food for a huge noisy family party. Grandmere, with busy work-chapped hands, would toil over an ancient stove whilst Grandpere, his white moustache yellowed in one corner from the ever present Gauloise clenched between his teeth, would open bottles of his 'special' wines and brandies.

These were the ones which had been lowered in crates into the millstream beside the house and hidden in a deep pool under the water-wheel throughout the war, to be raised again on VE Day by way of celebration. His eyes would twinkle and, as the bottles were emptied, the stories became wilder and the barracking noisier... until eventually Grandmere would sweep all the men out into the courtyard with her long-handled broom, leaving the women to gossip and clear away the debris.

At Giverny, Monet's garden was a profusion of colour, vibrant and gay. It was wonderful to see the water-lilies on the lake and the green bridge festooned in wisteria made famous in so many of his paintings. People of all nationalities swarmed through the gardens, bright as butterflies, fluttering and hovering between the flowers. The sound of motordrives of expensive cameras filled the air. Time to leave and head homewards for a few days in St. Ives and a visit to the Scilly Isles.

Whereas Monet was driven by the desire to capture the quality of light Walter Langley, founder of the Newlyn School of Artists, was interested in portraying the lives of simple working people, particularly fisherfolk, capturing the sadness and harshness of everyday life. At the Penlee Gallery in Penzance we saw a magnificent collection of his works with sad, emotive titles such as 'But men must work and women must weep' or 'The tender grace of a day that is dead will ne'er come back to me'. After the sunshine and 'joie de vivre' of Monet we were back to the gloom of our English summer.

The diversity of other people's creativity is always an inspiration. The gardens on Tresco did not exist 150 years ago and yet now, a sub-tropical wonderland of plants from South Africa, New Zealand and Madeira has evolved from the original plantings in bare rock. Brilliant flowers, monstrous agaves and towering echiums gave dramatic scale and height to a truly magical place.

The Minack Theatre is another remarkable achievement. To have created an amphitheatre, perched on the side of the cliffs, open to the elements and with the ocean as a backdrop, was a brave undertaking for anyone. Let alone a woman. Especially in an English climate. And yet the dedication of Rowena Cade has created an experience which is breathtakingly memorable. For me, Noel Coward's 'Blithe Spirit' has never had more charm than on that cool June evening with moonlight glittering on the water and the cold night air seeping slowly through my body.

Whatever the weather, there are so many wonderful English traditions that tell us it's Summer even when the skies are grey and overcast. We've shivered at Henley, been rained on at the Royal Show, enjoyed picnics and peaches, strawberries and champagne, fetes and family holidays, punting down the Cam watching the lawned gardens and historic colleges slide slowly by, choral evensong in Kings College Chapel, and choristers who sing like angels running home with their gowns flying and top hats tumbling off in the chase.

Claude Monet echoes my thoughts when in his letter to his friend Bazille he writes:

'Every day I discover more and more beautiful things. It's enough to drive one mad; I have such a desire to do everything, my head's bursting with it'.

10

Life goes too fast...

Life goes too fast. Already Autumn's rust is curling the edges of the sycamore and chestnut leaves. Squirrels are busy burying their nuts in instantly forgettable places and shiny conkers burst from spiky shells. Spiders' webs, bejewelled and shimmering with dew, spin out between the trees and, in the orchard, drowsy wasps suck sugar from fallen fruit. Our small birds are back at the feeders filling the air with cheerful song and badgers are destroying the lawn rooting out leather jackets, rather like pigs foraging for truffles. Summer is fading and leaves in invisible airy spirals snake slowly to the ground.

The peacocks have lost their fine tails and with them much of their arrogance. Their beautiful long feathers fall out one by one, leaving just a stumpy brown feathered tail through which the new season's finery will appear in the Spring. During this moulting period the birds are subdued, eating and sleeping to conserve energy for the winter ahead. Imran has fathered three chicks which Jemima has raised with admirable care. When she first escorted them to our door they were small and fluffy like little yellow ducklings. Now 8 weeks later they are about 12" tall with brown speckled and barred feathers like their mother, with just a hint of green and blue beginning to show through on their necks. We hope that at least two may be females so that Genghis will eventually have a mate of his own. Meanwhile he relies on Ducky Duck for friendship.

The fox left us with just one duck, a female Pochard, and a clutch of eggs, of which only one hatched. We call him Ducky Duck because at first we thought he was a she. He still has an identity problem. He looks like a cross between a mallard and a seagull, and thinks he is a peacock, spending his days with Genghis and presumably wondering when his legs will grow. He spends very little time on the pond being a duck and greets his friend with a delighted 'Mwack- mwack!' when he swoops down from his tree in the morning. He is so pleased to see Genghis that he runs over the lawn to greet him tripping over his big yellow flippers in his haste. Together they graze the garden and snooze on the warm gravel side by side.

Life goes too fast. Last week we visited one of our prettiest, kindest and most glamorous friends. She had shrunk almost beyond recognition, taken five hours to dress and prepare for our visit and, almost unable to breathe, had presided over an elegant tea reminding her daughter to provide pastry forks and only the best napkins. Five days later we attended her funeral at Dorchester Abbey. Friends who had decorated St. Paul's Cathedral and Westminster Abbey for the Royal weddings had filled the vast church with soaring arrangements of exquisite white lilies and sweet scented roses. 300 voices filled the air with her favourite hymns, their love for her reverberating from the ancient stones. Women wept and men looked sombre. Autumn sunshine slanted through tall windows onto her pale oak coffin. The Nunc Dimitis had never seemed more sad. I am reminded to treasure every single moment of my life. Good or bad, they go too fast.

And then, like a video clip, that scene is over and we're whizzing down the motorway to Devon listening to the demise of an American President, embarrassed by the invasion of his privacy. Freedom of information, the press, the media, the internet all encourage us to be judgemental. They invite opinion and provide a seedbed for bigotry. Are his critics so perfect themselves that they should delight in or decry his private weakness when his public role is beyond reproach? Fallibility is part of the human condition. I prefer it to the predictability of the zealot or the micro chip and even a micro chip is fallible sometimes...

It may be clever enough to programme our boiler or to launch a nuclear warhead but is apparently unable to understand the simple abbreviation of the year 2000. Incredible isn't it that we rational human beings have allowed ourselves to become so reliant on something so small, so all powerful.

And yet information technology has crept insidiously into our lives. Now, like Pavlov's dog we bow to its commands. '*Answer me!*' says the angry red eye on the answering machine. How can I refuse? '*Read my messages!*' says the fax machine with a reproachful green eyed stare. '*Insert more paper! Replace my ribbon!*' commands the word processor, refusing to continue unless I obey. '*You have messages*', says the invisible woman hiding in the carphone. '*You have messages – please call 121*'. And of course I do!

With the advent of digital TV even our television now asks '*Do you want to interact with me?*' No, of course I don't, I'm far too busy interacting with real live human beings, but I hardly dare say so in case it hears me and answers back!

The communications explosion of the 90's has certainly been amazing, with computers moving from main frame to laptop and even palm top, the advent of fax machines, mobile phones, e-mail, the internet and the proposed Ethernet but at the end of the day we are only human and there's a limit to how much communicating one wants to do in a day.

Life goes too fast. Already I'm suffering from communication overload. The phone rings continuously and my desk is stacked with unanswered letters. Mail order catalogues remind me that Christmas lurks around the corner and charities plead that they need my support. A communication from the taxman reminds me to self-assess or be damned. Barclaycard offers limits of credit with noughts so prolific one wonders if the printer has jammed. (If only my bank statement used the same printer!). But not to worry. I'll soon be able to escape from it all – Reader's Digest assures me that I, Prunella Dart, have been selected from a cast of thousands to be a (potential) millionaire. Did they tell you that too? If so, please don't tell me. Just for a moment I've found time to dream!

11

CHRISTMAS 1998

Deadlines are not my forte!

Deadlines are not my forte! My editor will verify that! I'm just not ready for Christmas, for trees and trimmings, parties and presents. It will have to be a last-minute affair. Simple, understated and meaningful. All the usual razzamatazz can wait until next year, to celebrate the Millennium. Meanwhile, the pudding's in the pantry, and the cake's in the tin, so it's really just the presents I have to choose and cards to send to faraway family and friends.

I have one very special friend. He's trustworthy, loyal and never lets me down. We're a great team. He's quite a bit younger than me. He's even good looking, although I guess we're both beginning to show our age a little now. But after all our years together it still gives me pleasure to see him across a crowded car park. My husband worries about us, especially when we're out late together and a long way from home, but he still trusts him. And late in the night, burning up the miles between far-flung destinations, I find his warmth and familiarity safe and secure.

An advert for Christmas presents said '*Send a friend to a Health Spa for a day of top to toe relaxation and beauty therapy.*' It sounded tempting. I booked my friend in without delay.

OK, so to you he's just a car, an old blue BMW with peacock scratches on his roof, but we've travelled 140,000 miles together without complaint in wet and wind, snow and sunshine, traffic jams and open highway. Despite a daily mud-pack and massage along our narrow country lanes he deserved a special treat. And sure enough, after a full day's top to toe pampering and special treatment for a small water retention problem, he reappeared purring with contentment, looking sleek, rested, and well groomed. Champney's would have been proud of the bill!

Thus rejuvenated we've been back tramping the highways, eating up the miles between work and duties, family and friends, creating our own special groove in the tarmac between Devon, London and Oxfordshire. Together we snarl at the number of roadworks that slow us down, and revel at the beauty of the autumn countryside that passes like videotape across the screen. Startling images flash by: golden leaves and scarlet berries against sharp blue skies; black storm clouds over dark ploughed fields; golden gingerbread houses in Cotswold villages huddled together in warm sunshine; beside the motorway vast modern warehouses teaming with activity, fleets of trucks loading at every door like piglets suckling milk from a sow.

In London squally winds peel sticky backed leaves from grimy, glutinous pavements to slap them coldly against one's legs. Grim-faced joggers, defying heart attacks, jostle walkers from their path and hard-eyed pigeons view one with intent.

Walking in a South London park can be, as we know from recent revelations in the Fleet Street scandal sheets, a perilous occupation. A notice by the lake advises against immersing oneself or one's pet in its foetid waters for fear of poisoning from toxic aquatic algae. Another exhorts us not to feed and thus encourage the wildlife as numbers already vastly exceed those capable of being supported by the natural habitat, causing the erosion of banks and the destruction of vegetation. Lest one should find other ways to amuse oneself a kill-joy notice advises that rollerblading is banned in the restaurant!

Had it been the Minister for Agriculture discovered here, rather than his soul-mate the Secretary for Wales, one could have assumed he was doing timely research into the disastrous effects of urbanisation of the countryside: pollution of waterways, transmission of disease, unsustainable wildlife, the pressures of public access, and the destruction of flora and fauna. Quite apart from vital food production for the nation, he might realise that without the voluntary efforts of Britain's farmers to maintain the countryside it will quickly decline into this kind of urban decay.

Instead, farmers across the nation battle for survival, for the right to sell their produce at a profit, to compete in a market stacked against them by trading agreements and a strong pound. It seemed appropriate that this year we celebrated Harvest Festival not in a small country church but in the vast church of St. Bartholomew the Great in Smithfield. It is sadly here, in the City of London, not in the wide open spaces of the shires that the future of farming is to be decided. I wish my husband would exercise his right as a Freeman of the City of London to drive a flock of sheep over London Bridge and bring the area to a standstill. Perhaps if politicians were unable to go about their business unhampered they might be more appreciative of the current restrictions faced by our farmers.

And whilst we produce more than we can sell, floods and famine sweep through central America, refugees hunt for food in the bitter cold of Kosovo, and Saddam stockpiles weapons of such massive destruction that the Middle East teeters on the brink of war.

So, if I could wave a magic wand, what would I give for Christmas presents this year? World peace, fair trade, relief from famine and disease, hope, respect for our planet and every living creature upon it, a sense of wonder at the beauty of life and, above all, love.

Or do you think they would prefer another tie or a pair of socks?

Happy Christmas!

12

Another New Year, another blank page…

———◆◈◈◈◆———

Another new year. Another blank page on which to write our dreams. Change is in the air. New hopes, new fears, new endings, new beginnings. The death of a century, the birth of a new millennium. The race is on, the countdown under way. Inexorably we are pulled to the brink of the year 2000 to hurl ourselves over its edge into the bottomless pit of our expectations.

Will we say farewell to the twentieth century with regret? Savour her last remaining days? Bury her with dignity? Eulogise her achievements? Or will we throw her on the scrap heap without a thank-you or a prayer and rush forward to embrace all that is new?

For suddenly everything is 'new'. New Labour, New Age, New Millennium, New Euro. 'New' somehow implies excitement and hope, but also something unproven, uncertain and potentially worrying. Certainly, whether we stand like Canute against the tide or let go and drift with the flow, change is inevitable. Some people find it harder to cope with than others. Increasingly, 'change counsellors' are required to help people reconstruct their lives after the traumas of redundancy, death, or illness.

For others it is the fear that the baby will be thrown out with the bath-water and that 'new' will not live up to its promise of being better than 'old'.

But we cannot hold on to the past however attached to it we may have become. Life sweeps us along on its roller-coaster ride and if we always travel with our back to the engine we will fail to see the new opportunities coming our way.

Feng Shui, the Chinese art of harmony and balance, makes use of the energy created by change to accentuate the positive in life, to help us create the life that we really want. The belief is that by creating a template of our hopes and aspirations in our immediate environment, the physical changes we make stimulate the relevant areas of our lives, to activate the changes we require – i.e. 'positive thoughts require positives actions'. To make room for these new opportunities we must first clear out all the clutter and stagnant energy that is holding us back. Feng Shui says '*If you don't love it, don't use it or if it doesn't bring you joy, get rid of it! Clearing clutter sets you free and allows new energy to enter your life*'.

The ancient Chinese accepted change as the natural cycle of Life and used its repeating patterns as recorded in the 'I Ching' or 'Book of Change' to understand the here and now and to divine future trends. Their aim was to find the 'Tao' or the 'Path' which would enable them to live in harmony with the times. Their philosophy provides a certain comfort by showing that we are part of a great design – that what we perceive as 'new' is really 'recycled'.

Europe now has the Euro and one suspects that before long Britain will join the common currency and, like it or not, will be sucked into the federalism of 'New' Europe, losing our autonomy and sovereignty in the process. One wonders how those families who lost husbands, sons and brothers in the wars to 'free' Europe must feel as we consider voluntarily handing over our power to Brussels and our gold reserves to the Bundesbank. For an island nation that has always been proud to be free it is an alarming, but seemingly inevitable prospect.

However, those of us who view the transfer of power to Europe and the adoption of a common currency with trepidation should take comfort from the events of 1700 years ago. With the Roman Empire in decline, its Emperors moved east, setting up a new power base in Byzantium, creating a glittering new civilization built to the glory of God. By charging ten per cent on all goods traded through their city they earned money to pay for their buildings, their public service and their entertainments. The value of the Byzantine coinage was so consistent that it became the international trading currency, and merchants from as far away as China preferred to use it rather than their own. (So nothing new about trading Euros on the Hang Seng.) The Emperor Constantine wanted to call his city New Rome, but it quickly became known as Constantinople. How long before Brussels is renamed New London, or perhaps Blairstadt or Tonyville?

And whilst our ministers are now tempted with Pugin wallpapers and interest-free loans, Emperor Constantine encouraged his with luxurious new villas built in the style of those in Rome. He also pacified the masses with "bread and circuses". A foretaste of sandwiches at the Dome?

As we lurch towards Europe, and worry about the cultural and economic changes the new millennium may bring, we should heed the words, found etched on a limestone slab in the city of Uruk, by a philosophical Sumerian: *'He who possesses much silver may be happy. He who possesses much barley may be happy. But he who has nothing at all can sleep'.* Or indeed: *'You can have a lord, you can have a king, but the man to fear is the tax collector'.* And finally (A personal favourite!): *'We are doomed to die. Let us spend!'.*

Those words were written 5,000 years ago.

Plus ca change!

With best wishes for a happy and eventful New Year!

13

MARCH 1999

Postcard from Paradise

—————◦◦◦————

Not so much 'Horswell Diary' as 'Postcard from Paradise'. For before the intrusion of tourism this small island (Koh Samui) off the east coast of Thailand must surely have been the Garden of Eden – a box of jewels more precious than any Maharani's dowry.

Set in a sea of turquoise flecked with gold, jade-fringed palm trees cast amethyst shadows over platinum sands. At night, stars glitter bright as diamond chips in soft sapphire skies. The whole island scintillates with colours, sights and smells that energise the soul. Everywhere there is a feeling of vibrancy, vitality and abundance – a celebration of Life itself.

Under the watchful eye and benevolent smile of the giant golden Buddha perched on a hilltop, the islanders live tranquil, harmonious lives in accordance with his teachings. Buddhism's benign respect for life, coupled with a sense of personal responsibility, or Karma, is reflected in every aspect of their lives. They know that to receive one must also give. No gift is accepted without the most gracious thanks. Nothing is taken without some small reciprocal offering being given. Each house, however humble, has at its entrance a miniature 'spirit house' richly decorated and garlanded with flowers. Here offerings of food and drink are left to feed the gods in return for their continuing bounty and protection.

Their own homes are built to embrace the elements. Traditionally thatched, raised on stilts to catch the breeze, steep roofs collect the monsoon rains for later use and overhang dark verandas giving precious shade. Vibrant flowers spill from terracotta pots clustered around their doors and lotus blooms float in idle waters. Songbirds in ornate wicker cages suspended from the eaves trill and coo as lean cats sidle snugly around open doorways. Amber-skinned children play nearby without malice or tears.

Everywhere one senses a happy symbiosis between man and nature. Perhaps it is still nature who is top dog, allowing man to live like a flea on its back – tolerated, though an occasional irritant, and in extreme cases, a risk to its overall well-being. Whilst nature's raw energy thrusts vast coconut palms and flowering trees upwards towards the sky, man pads quietly about his business in their shadows reaping their abundant fruits and giving thanks to his god.

Watching these shy gentle people being trained to cope with the unsmiling demands and ungracious behaviour of their cosmopolitan guests, it is easy to see that the world would be a better place if the roles were reversed and the guests could learn some of the calm, soothing sweetness of their Thai hosts.

With tourism comes, inevitably, commercialism, yet this too is effected with tolerance and humour. Market stalls are laden with riches harvested from local waters. Gleaming snapper, sea bass, shark, oysters, king prawns and lobsters nestle in sparkling ice. Fruit stalls are ablaze with colour, piled high with bananas, mangoes, papaya, lychees, limes and coconuts. Tie-dyed sarongs flutter bright as butterfly wings beside cooking utensils that clink together in the breeze, twirling on their strings. Delicate flowers carved from soap and boxes made from shells of abalone and pearl vie with fake 'designer' clothes to satisfy the tourist's hunger for a bargain whilst pineapples are crushed with ice and coconut milk to quench his thirst.

Tailors' shops overflow with silks that echo the blues of sea and sky, the greens of the rainforest, the vibrant pinks, oranges and purples of flowering bougainvillea and the rich golds and reds of an island sunset.

Language makes a mockery of well-intentioned signs. A menu invites one to enjoy 'grilled crad craw' and at the temple we are told that out of respect 'No wearing brassieres, close-fitting shorts or underpants allowed'. At night the street comes alive with lights and music, spicy cooking smells and tooting taxis. Tourists jostle happily with snake-charmers and street vendors, soothsayers and stallholders. Bargaining is fierce but agreement always reached with a smile. Transvestites, feathered and bejewelled like exotic birds, and with fantastic 'maquillage' invite one to their 'Folies Bergeres'. Buddhist monks in saffron robes offer redemption in old age when 'lady boy' can no longer trade on his cute androgeny.

To-day, my husband arrived from England with dismal tales of cold and sleet, monetary union and proposals for 76,000 new homes in Devon. I felt despair drop like a pebble in Utopia, rippling out across the surface of my island paradise.

14

May 1999

Home, Sweet Home…

———⊸◦◦◦⊸———

Anyone who has ever felt homesick will know the feeling when the very mention of the word 'home', like the clapper touching the sides of an enormous bell, resonates deeply through one's body. Gradually, the vibrations become a diminishing echo, receding to a ghostly whisper calling you back. Whatever reason one had for leaving, whatever problems one may have left behind are blurred in a golden haze of nostalgic euphoria. Home suddenly feels like the only place to be.

Returning to Horswell is like all those imagined homecomings rolled into one: The excitement of anticipation. Driving a little too fast along narrow lanes. Loosening one's seat belt ready to jump out of the car the moment it stops. Lowering the window to talk to the dogs as they gambol beside us escorting us up the drive. The peacocks yahooing their greeting from the treetops and Ducky waddling at speed across the lawn to beat us to the front door. The garden, more green and overgrown than when we left. Cherry trees, magnolia, camellias and rhododendrons laden with blooms. Family and friends waiting to greet us and a tea tray ready with cups of tea and home made cakes. Later there will be post to sort, calls to answer and duties to assume but for now there is just the glorious oneness of being home. A wandering spirit settling back into its material body.

But whilst we sip tea in English sunshine, Nato aircraft drop yet another payload of Bombs on Serbia as thousands of displaced Albanians continue to flee the traumas of Kosovo. These are people who look like us, dress like us, think and feel, bleed and cry like us and yet because of racism and the brutality that it begets, are people for whom the word 'home' currently has no meaning. Our Prime Minister boldly stated that these refugees will be able to return to their homes. But will they exist? What will they find? Without papers, what proof of ownership will they have? Can the scene of rape and murder of members of one's family be termed 'home' ever again? Will a beloved pet come up to them and lick their hand? Will a lost child appear from the rubble? Or a husband, once feared dead, enfold them in the comfort of his arms? The anguish is too great to imagine.

The world is like our garden. In some parts beautiful, in others a mess, never all perfect at the same time and without constant care, prone always to chaos. In some areas the occupants are happy to stand alone or entwine together in happy symbiosis, the strong supporting the weak. In others, usually where there is the best soil and the most precious plants, invasive weeds with relentless persistence prey on all that is beautiful and good. They stifle their very existence without any conscience whatsoever, greedily taking over their territory and the sustenance that it provides. Somehow, whatever the conditions, weeds seem always to thrive. That, I suppose, is why man has to dream up dreadful deterrents like Round Up and Gromoxone, Cruise Missile and Smart Bombs.

Whatever happened to tolerance, acceptance, mutuality? Does it really not exist? It seems that life is devolving into smaller and smaller factions with cultural and ethnic groups banding together for protection from persecution. Whether it is a nail bomb in London, or Milosevic in Kosovo, the real catalysts for destruction are zealotism and bigotry, narrow mindedness and greed.

If we are to prevent increased factionalisation in our own country through cultural intolerance, with Scotland and to a lesser extent Wales breaking away from England, the time has surely come for us to recognise our own multicultural society and weld it firmly into a cohesive, if colourful, Englishness, of which we can all be proud.

If we can get three dogs, seven peafowl and a duck to live happily together, and I see a black and gold hen has just appeared in their midst, presumably a refugee from next door, surely multi-culturism can work?

Perhaps what the world needs is a little Horswell magic!

15

July 1999

Living dangerously...

———◦◦◦———

At last Summer has arrived. Our feathered muezzins in their treetop minarets wake us early with their strident call to morning prayer. Warm stillness and a misty dawn show promise of another cloudless day. I try to keep my eyes closed against the light but dogs are clamouring for their early morning swim and my husband flaps a swimsuit above my comatose body to test for signs of life.

I'm tempted to react like a bull to a matador's cape but instead am soothed by a welcome cup of tea, the latest news bulletin and a weather report. In minutes I am careering down to the beach with a carload of yelping over-excited dogs. Any thoughts that I may still be dreaming are quickly dispelled by the sea's cold waters but, once in, it feels delicious and the difficulty is to drag oneself back to the realities of the day ahead. Even the dogs hang back for one last swim or one last throw of the stick before we reluctantly trundle home for breakfast smelling of salt and seaweed.

By now the peacocks have swept down from their night-time roost and are strolling around the garden looking for food. Ducky, our solitary drake, waddles along beside them quacking instructions; bossy as ever with his chest puffed out and the feathers on his deformed wing sticking up like a swagger-stick under a sergeant-major's arm.

46

One day the long suffering peafowl had obviously had enough of Ducky's persistent attention and turned on him, pecking him cruelly. Fearing for his life we chased his assailants away. To our surprise Ducky immediately rallied and waddled at speed after the largest cock-bird, grabbing the end of his tail feathers with his beak. Looking utterly amazed the peacock let out a loud squawk and, high-stepping through the long grass, started to run quickly away. Unabashed, Ducky hung on tightly, stuck his little orange feet out at a defiant angle and allowed himself to be towed around the orchard like a water-skier in a rough sea!

Recently the woods have been scented with the smell of fox. Dogs and peafowl sound the alarm when he's about and occasionally we see one hurrying guiltily through the garden. We hope that the peafowl will fly away in time or stay up in their roost but sadly poor Jemima was unlucky. She of the sweet temperament and brief sojourn on Thurlestone church tower. Proudly nursing her fluffy little pea-chicks she was no match for our wily dawn-raider. To the horrified shrieks of the other birds. Monsieur Renard dragged her away, leaving a swathe of feathers and four pathetic little chicks as a tragic memorial to her cruel demise.

We loved Jemima. She was sweet and shy and beautiful and a wonderful mother. She watched over her chicks constantly, allowing them to sleep nestled out of sight in the soft downy feathers beneath her wings. When awake she walked them around her domain, showing them their boundaries; where to find food and water and how to trust humans and dogs. She guided them with a series of simple clicking noises and always placed herself between them and any potential danger. She stayed with the three survivors of last year's brood right up until this year's mating season, guiding, teaching and protecting them all year. She died protecting this year's little family and all our feeding and care will never be able to compensate for Jemima's loving wisdom.

The garden is awash with roses making the surrounding disarray look almost intentional. Mauve-blue clematis tangle with pink roses and tumble through grey trellises. Green tentacles of wisteria and jasmine reach out to lasso tall spires of delphinium, phlox and campanula. Islands of pale catmint, dark lavender and pink cranesbill geraniums float on a foaming sea of lime green alchemilla mollis. Close one eye and it looks a dream. Open both and the workload is daunting.

Childhood memories of stately cedars on pale lawns silvered by moonlight have for years inspired the desire to plant a cedar of our own. But where? To find sufficient space to do justice to its wide-spreading branches is surprisingly difficult. The search for the perfect spot is rapidly degenerating into a typical divorce-inducing marital dispute, akin to picture-hanging, reversing the car, picking up boat moorings or discussing the mother-in-law. In fact the mother-in-law has been 'discussed' quite a lot lately as it was she who so generously gave us the tree in question!

No tree has been in and out of the ground more times than this. I have discovered that the words *'Actually, darling...'*, when preceded by a difficult but perfectly executed tree planting, can bring me closer to God than any other words in the English language.

Apparently, just as the last spadeful of earth is sprinkled around the plant a strange shifty sideways look takes over my face. Like a spectator at Wimbledon my head twists from side to side as I eye up a possible improvement to the selected site, visually weighing one position against the other. This, I am told, is then followed (just as the soil is tamped into place, the acheing back straightened and the tools cast aside) by *'Actually, darling... I think it might look better a little to the left/right... not much, just a couple of inches/feet/yards... honestly darling, not far.'*

I understand that I should be extremely grateful that the next hole that is dug is not 18' wide by 5'4" beneath a headstone engraved with my name.

But of course I should not be in it for long. *'Oh no darling, surely not there... maybe here... er, no, actually I think I might look better here... a little further to the left/right... Or perhaps over here?... What do you think?'*

16

A mirage of heat and dust

For me the words 'Indian Summer' conjure up a mirage of heat and dust, of golden light and sultry opulence. I see a slow procession of dusky figures draped in silks of saffron, amber, garnet and rust, borne on stately elephants and gaudy palanquins. Gently swaying in cushioned howdahs, I see Maharajahs twirl ornately tiered and tasselled parasols. Turbanned attendants waft peacock fans to stir the drowsy air and dark eyed beauties draw sequinned veils across their face revealing golden bangles on slender wrists. There is no sound as they pass by and disappear save the tinkle of harness and the weary shuffle of elephants' feet.

A scene too colourful perhaps to describe our English September, and yet it shares the languor and the dusty glamour of these golden autumn days: the richness of plump berries on the briar; the sated wasp drowning in the sweetness of an overripe plum; the lingering rose, heavy with perfume. The orchard trees are burdened with fruit and on larder shelves jars of homemade jam glow like lambent jewels.

Skeins of noisy geese in tight formation flap through the air as if on unoiled hinges and magpies cackle and squabble in the hawthorn tree.

49

Dragonflies hover in the still air and squirrels skip scatterbrained across the lawns. Leaves of sycamore and chestnut start to crisp and fall, and in the woods exotic toadstools suddenly appear.

Crane flies are coming indoors to dance their final frenzied jig and fading butterflies with folded wings prepare for Winter's rest. As in the mirage, there's a sense of distance travelled and journeys yet to come.

The dogs and I are still swimming at the beach although the air is often chill and strands of weed slither snake-like around us in the water. Bertie the Briard is nervous of swimming out of his depth and pleads with our poor old arthritic Labrador to retrieve his stick if it floats out too far. Abo is happy to oblige, proudly showing his superior skills to the younger dog, but suffers dreadfully from aching joints once back on dry land. Flossie the sheepdog has to be bribed from the water with the promise of food before I turn blue waiting for her.

Jemima's three pea-babies had grown fit and strong and now reside at Woodlands Country Park. I am sure they will find living alongside ostriches and llamas far more exotic than with three dogs, two humans and a duck. With mating and moulting finished the remaining peafowl are strangely quiet, but eating voraciously to build up strength for the cold months to come. Campanulas are their particular favourite. Under attack from alarming numbers of rabbits and now peafowl the wire around our garden is increasingly resembling the perimeter fence at Colditz.

There is comfort in the rhythms of the seasons, a familiarity that marks our passage through time and space. But Autumn is a mystery, an act of faith embodied in the fragrant incense of garden bonfires. It asks us to believe that after the dormancy of Winter, life will be renewed in the Spring. I wonder, does the hibernating bat or the pupating butterfly know for sure that it will wake up or be transformed? Does the dormant daffodil ever doubt that it will reappear next Spring? Is the squirrel really storing nuts for the following season or is he, like the ancient Egyptians, making provision for his journey to an afterlife? In Autumn we pledge our faith in the future through the ritual preparations for the coming season; raking and burning fallen leaves, stacking logs; trimming and pruning and putting our gardens to bed for their long Winter's sleep When the new shoots appear we will be at the start of a whole new Millennium.

Meanwhile, let us enjoy our 'Indian Summer'. Let us linger in the sunshine, savouring its richness and beauty, committing every glorious detail to memory before the days shorten and the light dims on the last Autumn of the 20th Century. Let us reflect on the distance we have travelled, and look forward to the journeys yet to come.

17

CHRISTMAS 1999

A break from tradition?

———◦◉◦———

Christmas, usually a time steeped in tradition, is just around the corner, but this year, with the new Millennium appearing over the horizon, there's a sense of breaking with the past and stepping, somewhat uncertainly into the new.

In the words of the old Bob Dylan song, 'The times they are a-changing'. And changing fast. Too fast perhaps for some people's liking; the different ideology too hard to grasp, the break with lifelong traditions uneasily accepted.

Hunting, Hereditary Peers, Lay Magistrates all being axed; British agriculture handed wholesale to our competitors in Europe. The destruction of country life. The Queen being considered too English to remain Head of the Commonwealth. The National Anthem too frumpy for the revellers at the Dome.

Black Rod, too intimidating for new ministers, the muffling of citizens demonstrating against civil rights abuse during the State Visit from China. Publicly disgraced Ministers returning to the Cabinet. Our Laws overturned by a foreign Court. Is this the England that we know and love?

One wonders if the ravens on our chimney are deserters from the Tower, an early warning that the country is indeed in danger. Should we feel threatened by the changes to our great British heritage? Or do we accept that we are entering a new age, a new attitude, an impersonal egalitarian era of technology and political correctness?

Pioneers throughout the centuries, motivated by the narrow restrictions of life at home through poverty, the need to conform to a rigid Establishment or, in some cases, religious persecution, broke away to establish new communities with a new freedom of spirit. Their departure from the stifling attitudes of their day gave them a fresh start, a break from outmoded tradition, a chance to rewrite the rules and find endless scope for growth and new ideas.

History repeats itself. Now, with electronic information and e-commerce accessible via the internet, there are again fantastic discoveries to be made and vast empires to be built. This time the new colonies are in Cyberspace and our brave young pioneers are already amassing great fortunes through staking an early claim to their territories.

In times gone by such wealth was only available to the few intrepid explorers, pioneers, merchants, miners, opportunists and privateers, who forsook the safety of the known world to seek new frontiers and extend the boundaries of accepted beliefs, often at great risk to their credibility and personal safety. Now, with the advances in communications, the massive explosion of information technology has given millions of people access to extensive information and trading networks, without leaving the comfort of their homes. For those prepared to use it to their advantage the gains are immeasurable and the old barriers of class and creed non-existent.

New web sites are being registered daily, facilitating a global trade of information and goods unimaginable just decades ago. To those not yet conversant with the Internet the whole concept of websites and electronic trading is as illusory and incredible as were tales of arms dealing with African tribesmen when related in the comfort of overstuffed Victorian sitting rooms. And yet every day, new frontiers are being crossed and new previously unimaginable territories are being claimed creating a wealth of new ideas and opportunities.

So if we drag our feet in the rush towards the new Millennium, worrying what the new age will bring, perhaps, as we decorate our homes with holly and ivy in the centuries old way, we should drink a toast to these New Colonials and hope that the positive benefits of their daring departure from the world as we know it will outweigh the unseemly destruction of our ancient traditions.

After all, in the computer generated world of Virtual Reality there is life beyond death. Viscount Exmouth who lost his seat in the Lords reshuffle is setting up a website for discarded Hereditaries, creating a virtual House of Lords where he and his colleagues can continue to hold debates and take votes, the results to be published as an alternative to the real second chamber! Proving that, should life in the new Millennium not be entirely to our liking we can always create a more satisfactory version in Cyberspace and invite all our favourite people to join us there.

Whilst we turn our thoughts towards Christmas parties and Millennium Champagne our furry and feathered friends seem oblivious to such festivities, the dogs preferring a good squirrel chase and the peafowl eating everything in sight to prepare for a long winter. Only Abo, our ancient and adored Labrador seems to have shown any interest in the momentous occasion. Almost immobilised by arthritis but not wanting to be left behind in an increasingly technological age he has succeeded in getting himself micro chipped! It's a long story, best forgotten, involving dustbins, dog wardens and the threat of a large fine, which will no doubt feature strongly in his increasingly adventurous memoirs. Having previously returned home in a red Porsche and on another occasion, a pale blue Mercedes, one can only imagine that he mistook the warden's uniform for that of a liveried Chauffeur. Sadly we've discovered that the micro chip is not programmable to bring one's slippers or the newspaper, it simply means that the dog warden knows exactly where to collect the next fine. So much for progress!

Needless to say we are delighted to have Abo home, from where he joins me, my husband, Bertie the Briard, Flossie the Collie, 6 peafowl and Ducky in wishing you all a wonderful Christmas and an exciting new Millennium!

18

JANUARY 2000

Influenza? Or the Millennium Bug?

All the hype over the Millennium celebrations has produced a plethora of statistics: the number of visitors to the Millennium Dome; the number of hours they had to wait for entry; the size of the crowds lining the Thames to watch the fireworks; the number of hot dogs consumed and the millions of pounds spent/wasted on the whole event.

But what interests me is how many zillions and squillions of micro-bes were transferred in that one ecstatic inter-millennial kiss? For in that single moment of New Year euphoria the much vaunted, although clearly misunderstood Millennium Bug seized the day and in- filtrated the unguarded systems of the nation. With D Day precision and computers as their decoy, they swarmed through the people's unmanned defences to seize the country quite literally by the throat. Under cover of fatigue and hangovers the vile intruders made good their initial assault, digging in and preparing their artillery. By day two of the new Millennium the country awoke to the full extent of the takeover, finding themselves under attack and behind enemy lines.

A full scale alert, but 'not an epidemic' was announced, igniting our Bulldog spirit. The counter attack got under way. Hospitals opened their doors to the most serious cases, pharmacists dispensed tinctures and tablets, whilst the nation hacked and wheezed, coughed and spluttered, groaned and moaned, gazing at one another with rheumy eyes and discussed symptoms with voices hoarse and cracked. With communication severely impaired by these viral intruders, seasonal greetings became scrambled and incoherent. 'Habby Dew Year!', 'Habby Middeddium!', 'Like a dink?' 'Yeb please' 'Lemsip or cough mixture?' 'Would you like dat shaken or stirred?' As before when faced with a common enemy we found ourselves marching shoulder to shoulder to defeat the foe, united in our misery.

Of course, I have not got anything as common as a cold or as unsociable as flu. I cannot be seen to be ill or I will not be allowed to visit my husband in hospital for fear of spreading 'The Bug'. So, I blame my lack of voice on too many carols, my pink ferret-y eyes and feverish brow on an allergy to dust or hair of the cat. I tell myself I am fine and soldier on, determined not to give house room to a vagrant virus looking for a cosy billet. Why 'hair of the cat' you may wonder? A new addition to the Horswell menagerie? Well, no. To enable me to visit my ailing husband in Oxford, my mother and I have swapped houses. In doing so, she has acquired three well behaved dogs(Well, give or take the odd incident. More of that later!) and I have inherited one handsome, unbiddable, autocratic cat. (No comment about animals taking after their owners allowed.) I am allergic to cats. He knows that, waits until I'm asleep and then curls up on my head like Davey Crocket's hat. If I banish him from the room he takes revenge by clawing up the carpet outside my door, a sound that sears my nerves. If I put him outside he bides his time, waits until I am asleep, then jumps through an open window with a noisy thud and rewards my horrified squeal with a dead mouse.

Michael, meanwhile, lies in his hospital bed. Beneath his oxygen mask he looks like a tired traveller from outer space. Coloured liquids enter and leave his pale body through clear tubes coiled like tentacles around him. Monitors blip and scan. Nurses observe and record. I ask him about his journey and weary eyes signal that it is, at this stage, simply enough to have returned. The surgeon regards my cough with disdain, accepting my dust/cat's hair explanation with a withering look of despair. He considers me completely unscientific. As one of the country's most eminent Orthopaedic surgeons, I suppose that is his prerogative, although I do play up to it a bit. Perhaps I did go a little too far in my last thank you letter to him when, having performed a miraculous bone graft and hip replacement on my husband, I remarked that 'it was amazing what could be achieved these days with wing of bat and eye of newt'.

I also made the mistake of telling him about my forays into the world of Chinese medicine. How, having been given 7 brown bags containing a collection of funghi, herbs, bark and other unidentifiable bits of skin and bone to boil up into the most foetid, rancid stew it occurred to me that having just paid my annual subscription to the Save the Tiger fund I was probably undermining my own contribution by boiling up the very bones of my adopted tiger! This proved too much for the poor man who, with a look at his Registrar that said 'You see the kind of cranks I have to deal with', swept off to see his next patient. It was, perhaps, a good thing that I did not complete my story for having been unable to stomach the vile brew for more than a day, the remaining 6 bags of dry ingredients were left untouched on the dresser in the kitchen. When I last spoke to my mother on the telephone, towards the end of our conversation she added 'Oh by the way, I saw you'd bought that special compost so I've repotted the six orchids in the hall'.

Christmas preparations were a mixed blessing for the Horswell hounds. A constant stream of visitors denied them their usual place in front of the Aga or an open fire. Tinsel collars and Bonios did little to relieve their gloom when banished to their baskets. However, on Christmas morning they joined us in front of a blazing fire to open presents. A wonderful dog-loving friend had made all of the dogs a Christmas stocking, each with its own card and special message. e.g. 'to Dear Abo with love from Auntie Marge. See you soon so don't run away!' Flossie's pointed nose meant she could dive straight in and retrieve a new ball with her name on it. Abo's greed meant he ripped the whole stocking apart in his haste to gobble down the Chummy Chew lurking in the toe, and Bertie's bewilderment at being given anything so exciting sent him running around the room tossing the whole thing repeatedly in the air, delighting in every treat as it tumbled out on to the floor.

Bertie is not really a party animal. Crackers terrify him; fireworks are his idea of hell. To get him through the Millennium celebrations the Vet prescribed sedatives to calm him. This necessitated a visit to the surgery, so off we went. It was like walking into a scene from Doctor Doolittle; the room so crowded that people and animals seemed piled up on top of one another, a chaotic jumble of dogs and cats, rabbits, guinea pigs, a parrot in a cage and an oil covered guillemot. Bertie behaved impeccably. Well, that's if you discount attacking the Vet, biting his stethoscope and refusing to be examined. Suffice to say our departure was hasty and the pills worked, but poor Bertie's New Year hangover looked even worse than ours.

For me, the party atmosphere of the last few weeks has kicked off the New Year to a flying start. I'm full of hope and expectations for the year ahead, excited by the sheer pleasure of being alive. What greater gift can there be than a whole new year of opportunities? It's so great you cannot measure it, so diverse you cannot quantify it, so variable you cannot contain it, the potential for transformation endless and unimaginable. A new year is so precious you cannot begin to estimate its value. It even comes gift wrapped with snowdrops and aconites, birdsong and moonbeams, starlight and twinkling hoar frost, early daffodils and rich camellias. It's priceless, available to everyone and, amazingly, it's free! As with any gift, although given with the greatest love and optimism, the donor cannot be sure that it will be fully appreciated. There is always the fear that it may be considered worthless and treated with contempt. But this year especially, at the start of a new Millennium He must surely hope that we recognise our exceptional good fortune. Happy New Year!

19

MARCH 2000

The ghosts of Horswell

—⊳◉◉◉⊲—

The ghosts of Horswell obviously felt that we had been away for too long. They are possessive of our time, feeding on our energy to keep their home alive. No longer able to perform the physical tasks necessary to maintain the beauty of their earthly paradise they look to us, the current guardians of their sanctuary, to toil and tidy, protect and preserve their status quo.

Unsettled by our long departure they have made their feelings known. Instead of the usual smile that greets us as we hasten up the drive, the house looked sullen, unforgiving, the grounds wintry, littered with debris from passing storms.

Rooms that had been unused in our absence lay thick with dust, sprinkled with dead flies. Salt laden raindrops smeared the windows and spiders' webs laced their frames.

Blocked drains had required massive subterranean explorations. These in turn had disturbed a hitherto unknown population of mice, who by way of reprisals ransacked the larder. Ratman was called; bait was laid.

The resulting odour became so vile and pungent it swamped our senses, stifling our breath with its venomous stench.

Dogs, already missing their walks with 'Auntie' Marge, lay low in their baskets watching us with reproachful eyes, whilst peafowl plucked desultorily at the remaining snowdrops snapping their stems.

Our home seemed lifeless; tired. I felt it waiting to feed on our energy, waiting for us to breathe it back to life.

Forty-eight hours earlier I had been walking along a white sand beach, huge turquoise rollers crashing beside me, dissolving in warm frothing foam around my feet. I had walked back along paths of perfumed gardenias to eat mango and pineapple for breakfast with friends. I wanted to turn back the clock, run away, leave the grey sky, the cold wind, the vile smell, the grumpy ghosts. Run before they seeped into me; stealing all the sunshine that I had stored up inside.

They read my mind. Panicking that their energy supply might slip from their grasp, they determined not to let me go. In desperation they released all the microbes they had kept from me over Christmas. Then, they had wanted to keep me fit and healthy. They love a good party. Lights, candles, hustle, bustle, laughter and chatter are all high-octane energy for ghosts to feast on. But now it was different. For several days they kept me weak and pathetic in my bed, stealing my energy whilst I slept.

Knowing I lay dreaming of Australian sunshine they turned their poisonous breath on my husband, to occupy me with his care.

Gradually, as the rhythm of the days fell into a familiar pattern, the ghosts relaxed their anxious vigil and returned to their shadows, feeling guilty perhaps for their tantrums and doubts that we would return.

Like a child shyly seeking forgiveness by offering to share its favourite toys, each day we were presented with a new and delightful treasure to remind us of the special beauty here. We were shown the apple-blossom blooms of early clematis, purple crocus and pale pink bluebells, croaking jackdaws dropping twigs down chimneypots and a blackbird's nest in the old box hedge.

The sun came out; vast patches of blue sky nudging away the gloomy grey. The lawns were mown releasing the delicious scent of fresh cut hay from the coumarin oil in the sweet vernal grass. The window cleaner arrived, more welcome and unexpected than the first cuckoo, to wipe away winter's tears and restore the house's smiling face. The foetid smell disappeared and busy hands brought back the sparkle to dusty rooms, filling them with daffodils and the scent of polish.

Now the camellias are all in flower; a profusion of pinks and reds. Some are single like large dog roses, exposing a cluster of golden stamens in their open palms. Others are frilled and fancy like a ballerina's skirt. Exotic magnolias have burst out from their drab brown disguise revealing a seductive display of milky white flesh.

Primroses form pale yellow cushions of dew-fresh blooms around the base of woodland trees and dark sweet violets shelter beneath their green umbrellas. On mossy banks fritillaries of white and mauve hold up their fragile bells and erythronia, like dainty witches' hats, rise up from darkly freckled leaves. At night the quarter moon shines so clear and bright one fears a frost yet revels in her beauty. The sky glitters with a million constellations – a textbook of astronomy.

In the morning one could be forgiven for thinking the whole galaxy had fallen to earth as yellow daffodils twinkle like golden stars in the darkness of the woods and pale anemones like asterisks attract the watchful eye. Squirrels chase small songbirds from their peanuts: They ooze over the bird-table like big grey slugs to hang by a tail and grab the feeders that swing below. We chase them away and wait for the return of our long tailed tits, blue tits, coal tits, greenfinch, robins and woodpeckers.

The peacocks' new tails are fully grown now and they look magnificent – easily eight feet wide when fully displayed. We have taken all the younger birds to Paignton Zoo where they will be able to fly freely among the other animals and roost at night in tall trees. Our remaining three birds – Imran, Genghis and Betty – are so much a part of our family now we would hate to lose them – but we are rather hoping that Betty is past the breeding age!

My husband has resumed his affair with Otter Nurseries (or is it Rose who works there?) returning with carloads of camellias, so one can only conclude he is well on the road to recovery from his two hip operations, which is a huge relief. The dogs have stacked their 'Bring Back Marge' placards in a corner and gone back to chasing squirrels and disappearing down rabbit holes. Ducky has fallen in love with a visiting Mallard, our days spent gardening are beginning to show results, the Spring sunshine seems here to stay and some semblance of normality seems to have been restored.

At last, all the spirits here at Horswell are once again in harmony and at peace.

20

MAY 2000

Is there any time more English than England in May?

⟫⟫◉◉◉⟪⟪

Is there any time more English than England in May? The heavy air, dense with moisture and the threat of thunder lulls one into dreamy indolence as we wait and hope for Summer to arrive. In city and in countryside pendulous racemes of trailing wisteria drip from mellow walls and clusters of richly scented lilac blooms release their heady perfume on the evening air. Suburban laburnums and sky blue jacaranda recall their days with the Raj when gin slings and tea and freshly squeezed limes were served with style beneath their cool branches and exotic blooms.

It's been a busy month of celebrations, anniversaries, birthdays, christenings and arrivals from overseas. A brief visit from my sister who lives in New Zealand means trying to cram eight years absence into just a few days. The last time she saw Horswell it was the bare and vandalised shell that we had bought at auction so it was exciting for her to see the difference now. The blazing colours of Azaleas and Rhododendrons remind her of her home and make me long for the bright blue New Zealand skies instead of our continuing cloudy grey.

We walk together, with the dogs, on Dartmoor, chattering every step of the way. New born foals sidle up against their mothers as we pass and rough coated cows lie quietly in grassy glades. The recent rains have created crystal rills that drip and tumble over mossy rocks as they make their way down to the valley below and the hills are covered with golden gorse. Bertie and Flossie gallop ahead enjoying their freedom and feeling the wind in their fur whilst Abo struggles to keep up. He takes his time, stopping to sniff for rabbits and to catch his breath. When the effort is too great he lowers his aching joints into a brackish puddle to cool the pain. His old white whiskered face seems to grin from ear to ear as he sinks into the oozing black mud with a contented sigh.

In London we visit the Chardin exhibition at the Royal Academy and the Art Nouveau at the V & A and later marvel at Maggie Smith's performance in Alan Bennett's play 'The Lady in the Van', – an absolute must for theatre goers! From our cabin on the London Eye we see the River Thames twist and turn from Lambeth Bridge to the Greenwich Dome. Familiar landmarks like St. Paul's Cathedral and Nelson's Column appear so small they could be miniature carvings on a Japanese netsuke. Listening to the comments of foreign visitors it is hard not to be proud of this great city and its centuries of history. Later, when seen from the river, even the irrelevance of the Dome has a place in our cultural and architectural heritage. Although its appalling cost should never be condoned, its structure and design is innovative and stylish. Very few passengers disembark to visit the Dome. Instead, we empathise with the nurses who hold placards demonstrating how many hospital beds could have been provided for the £950 million spent already on this huge white elephant.

Returning upstream we pass the old Naval College at Greenwich where the previous week my husband and I had attended a magnificent banquet for 400 people in the ornately decorated Painted Hall. Long tables laden with silver candelabra stretched the length of the vast hall, their white damask cloths starched and crisp. Glasses and silverware polished and gleaming reflected the sunlight that streamed in through tall cathedral windows, against which the sombre 'trompe l'oeil' paintings on the walls looked dark and rich. A band of the Royal Marines played as we entered and soon the room came alive with echoed conversations and reverberating laughter. After the meal Christopher Patten, accompanied by his wife Lavender, spoke movingly of his retreat from Hong Kong and one could not help but feel a sense of regret that the shifting sands of time are gradually eroding the history and traditions of this once great nation.

In Hampshire for the christening of our youngest twin grandsons we see cattle wading knee high in buttercup meadows, tugging with their rough tongues at long lush grass. In orchards, apple blossom lies deep as snow on gnarled branches casting dappled sunlight on sleeping sheep. Cow parsley foams and froths on green waves of roadside grass submerging campions and bluebells beneath its fragile filigree and cowslips stand singly on grassy banks. Splashes of yellow oil seed rape enrich the patchwork of the fields whilst its pollen, dry and dusty, irritates our nose and eye. In bluebell woods fresh green leaves of early beech hang soft and moist upon the bough while the underrated hawthorn bush hides its rural simplicity beneath a bridal veil of finest lace to beguile us with its beauty.

A 50th birthday party in an ivory tower near Exeter was a perfect finale to a perfect month, an opportunity to gather together friends and family from across the country and around the world. When we arrived at night, the rain was sleeting against the walls and fog pressed tight against the Gothic windowpanes but fortunately by morning the rain clouds and mist had rolled away. The 360 degree views from the Haldon Belvedere sweep across Dartmoor, Exeter, Exmouth, Torquay and all the way down to Cornwall. It is a magical place, a folly and a fantastic launch pad for my next half century!

21

JULY 2000

I believe in miracles…

⤜⟨◉◉◉⟩⤛

From the far side of the lawn our herbaceous border looks a sugar-spun confection of pale pinks and blues, greys, greens and white. Trailing clematis scatter butterfly kisses of purple and mauve across trellises laden with blue solanum and pink sweet pea. Roses and jasmine sway together like lovers, their fingers entwined, each in the other's hair. Jealously, Wisteria insinuates her lithe and supple body between them, using the wind to tug and prise them apart. From that distance the devastation wrought by plagues of rabbits cannot be seen. Even the docks and willow herb add to the charming profusion of leaf and flower.

I should be out there weeding and wonder why I permit myself such neglect. I blame it on the continuing gloom of our long awaited Summer. My energy is solar powered. Without blue skies and sunshine my batteries are running low. As I write, mist and clouds hang heavily above the trees with rain and cold winds forecast for the coming week.

It was the same weather in France. We celebrated my husband's birthday in the Loire Valley with all the family: 8 adults and 8 children from 18month old twins upwards.

Everyone made a huge fuss of the Birthday boy and the hotel created the most exquisite cake especially for him. Cutting into such creative perfection seemed as wantonly destructive as defacing a canvas by Watteau or Fragonard. No wonder they say the English abroad are vandals.

Remembering the glum reaction to one rather practical birthday gift – a dozen fruit trees that then required planting in rock hard soil and watering for the rest of the summer – I felt that this year a little whimsical indulgence might be more readily appreciated. So I gave him that most useful of presents, an item which no gentleman should ever be without: A solid silver boiled-egg cutter! Particularly useful in France where they neither eat boiled eggs for breakfast nor serve them upright in egg cups! Nevertheless, he was delighted.

Mechanised egg decapitation is about as far down the line as my husband is prepared to venture in this modern world of high technology. Although, in a moment of inspired generosity, he had bought me a computer for my birthday, it was an action which it would appear he now regrets. Not only does it occupy half his desk but he undoubtedly regards it as the enemy – an alien intruder that has taken over his wife's brain with the same ruthless speed and efficiency with which he can now lobotomise an egg. Whilst, as yet, he has not broken into a full frontal feathered fandango, he clearly views its presence with the same alarm and aggression as an angry peacock defending its territory.

'How,' he asks, 'despite all the hype, is it actually going to improve our lives?' I wax lyrical about e-mail, e-purchasing, information highways, word-processing, household accounts etc. 'Yes, but does it DO anything?'

'What do you mean?'

'Well, does it cook, or make beds, or do the shopping or clean the house??'

This is male-speak for 'You are wasting time. Now that you have Tiny to talk to, I am neglected.'

'But Darling, it's so exciting. Look! I've had e-mails from Brisbane, Perth, New Caledonia, Egypt, Washington, Auckland...'

'Pwooof!'

For the uninitiated, 'Pwoof' is male-speak for 'B——- (Bother) the rest of the world, the dogs need a walk.' It's a powerful expression, used in extreme conditions and guaranteed to send a mouse scurrying to the Log-off / Shut-down icon immediately.

Actually, dog walking is a rather pleasant alternative at this time of the year. The lanes are full of moths and insects and butterflies dance over the hedgerows. The verges are tall with meadowsweet, hog weed and wild yellow mustard, whilst purple vetch and sweet white honeysuckle tangle with the dog roses on the briar. Abo's slow and painful progress gives me ample time to search for four-leafed clovers, a childhood obsession I've never been able to lose. I seem to find them with unnatural ease and feel, irrationally, that for me they truly are harbingers of good fortune. At home they fall from books where they have lain pressed and half forgotten between the pages. If not really 'lucky' in themselves perhaps they just remind me to be grateful for all the little miracles that come my way.

Thinking of miracles, several years ago when Abo was a young, sleek gun-dog, he and his litter-brother Alfie slipped away from the farm where my husband had been working, for a spot of illicit duck hunting. They did not return and could not be found. It was a black wintry night and pouring with rain. Eventually we called the police to report them missing. Almost immediately they called back to say that a shiny black dog had been killed on the busy main road beside the farm and was obstructing the road. Would we please go and remove the body. We were just leaving the house when the telephone rang again. It was the police saying that a second dog had been hit and was presumed dead, and again was obstructing the speeding traffic. They agreed to meet us there.

I think we drove the hour long journey in fifteen minutes, praying that it was all a big mistake and could not be true. On arrival the police protected us from the oncoming traffic, the reflective stripes on their car garish in the headlights, as we searched for their bodies. We found a large pool of dark blood near the side of the road but no dogs. Perhaps they are still alive, I ventured, maybe only stunned? The policemen shook their heads kindly. It was not possible. Their reports said otherwise. The hectic speed of the continuous traffic made me realise I was clutching at straws.

They suggested we came back in the daylight. We drove slowly home. The whole way back I railed at God, berating him for this injustice. I was so disgusted with Him I swore I'd never talk to Him again. And who was

He anyway to let a thing like this happen? If He was so blooming marvellous He had better make them both alive again.

Nobby, one of our farm managers, a man of few words and with a giant's heart, offered to go instead of us. He knew the area well. He rang mid morning to say he had found Alfie. My heart sank. I asked if he was badly injured. The answer was 'Yes. A terrible head wound.' At least, I thought, death would have been quick. I asked him to bring Alfie home. I wanted to bury him under the apple tree in the garden where he would be close to me. Nobby replied that the dog was already in the back of his van. That amazingly he had jumped in 'no trouble at all!'

'Jumped?' I asked, incredulous. 'You mean he's alive?'

'Oh yes,' said Nobby. 'So's the other one. I found them asleep in the barn.'

So miracles do happen, sometimes when you least expect them!

22

September 2000

Un coup de foudre

———◆◈◆———

O.K. so maybe I should not have poked fun at my husband's dislike of computers nor his penchant for lobotomy. Retribution was swift and unexpected, silencing my cyber-friend Tiny as effectively as a Russian Doctor's syringe in the arm of a grieving widow as she witnessed the authorities' disturbing failure to rescue her husband from the sinking Kursk submarine.

How was I to know my husband had friends in such high places? Even so, I do think a bolt of lightening might have been a little extreme. As a result poor Tiny has suffered a complete nervous breakdown and acute brain damage.

So here I am, packing up my traumatised new friend and sending him back to his maker for major brain surgery and a new modem implant – none of which I may say, surprise, surprise, is covered by B.U.P.A or whichever health scheme we purchased with him at the time. Our lack of communication is lonely and distressing. We had been getting on so well. Too well, my husband might say, almost inseparable. Now, suddenly, poor Tiny cannot even remember his name and seems in such a deeply catatonic state that he is totally unaware of my anxious vigil. I've even tried playing him his favourite CD's in the hope of some glimmer of recognition, but all to no avail.

Fortunately there are no waiting lists at the Tiny hospital and parts are readily available. (Forcing me to reassess my feelings about cloning). His return home is scheduled for next week, hopefully having made a full recovery.

Guests from France arrive to-day so I have been busy preparing a guest bedroom. The four poster bed has been made up with our best lace-edged linen and all cobwebs and flies removed from the light fittings and high ceilings. I'm assuming that since they are on honeymoon the ceilings may come under more detailed inspection than usual. Apart from lavender scented sheets, thick fluffy towels, fresh soaps, perfumed candles and fragrant flowers I am wondering what else I can provide to make their honeymoon suite more sumptuous. If they were English a well stocked drinks tray and a good selection of novels would surely suffice. But alas, they are French, causing my mind to boggle at the possibilities.

Looking for inspiration I recall those classic black and white art movies of my student days in Paris – films in which torrid love affairs, recorded in grainy celluloid, tantalised the cinematographic voyeur with their slow moving eroticism. Brief hesitant words laden with meaning, such as 'I love you', 'He's found out', 'He's got a gun'. 'I cannot leave you' would be punctuated by long tension-filled pauses and lingering camera shots of lipstick-ringed cigarettes burning to ash beside a half- finished glass of wine, whilst raindrops slithered slowly down the window pane. It was always the afternoon, always in someone else's apartment, always a sense of impending departure and always raining. Rain. That's obviously my missing ingredient!

Personally, I don't think rain is remotely romantic. During our recent week in Ireland it rained every day, transforming the scenery into watery landscapes with lakes, mountains and peat bogs etched against dark thunderous skies. We sheltered in simple farmhouses bright with flowers and crumbling stately piles filled with glorious Georgian antiques. Fortunately everywhere we went from Dublin to Connemara the welcome was warm and gracious, easily compensating for the chilly mists that seeped into our bones.

We returned home to find our house sitters stretched out on our new terrace, sipping Gin and Tonics in the sun and wondered briefly why we had ever left. Summer if we've actually had one seems to have been a see-saw event veering between drought and deluge. The garden has never been greener but flowers are now in short supply and signs of the changing seasons are beginning to appear: Voles are busy extending their labyrinthine tunnels beneath the lawn and badgers dig for crane-fly larvae under the cork oak tree. Conkers, like a spiked gladiator's mace, bristle on the chestnut trees and overnight, mushrooms push their snowy domes through dew laden grass.

High on the TV aerial house martins, jittery with excitement, surf the net for travel information and discuss their flight plans in high pitched voices.

Buzzards mewl and swoop above the trees and Jackdaws squabble on the chimney pots. Tawny owls pierce the night with their strident call and a watery halo around the moon speaks of rain.

In the lanes, Herb Robert, Cranesbill and the yellow spires of Common Toadflax try to brighten the dowdy hedgerows whilst pink and white striped cones of bindweed trail through yarrow, plantains, docks and thyme like strings of gaily painted fairy lights. Yet all their efforts cannot conceal the rusting dinginess of approaching Autumn.

Thinking of Autumn, I forgot to say that our honeymooning couple are both in their late seventies which surely proves that life is not without its surprises. They said that when they met it was a real 'coup de foudre' – literally a 'clap of thunder' or 'a bolt of lightening'.

Could this mean my computer is not brain damaged at all, but has simply fallen in love?

23

CHRISTMAS 2000

Storms and the unexpected

Compared with the devastation wrought by storms and floods in other parts of the country, we have been very fortunate. Even so, at the height of the gales, we feared for our trees as they thrashed and clawed at the demons tormenting them. The winds screamed through the woods, wrenching limbs and leaves from the trees, and slammed into the front of the house with relentless force. Pictures and furniture rattled against the walls despite their immense thickness and windows thundered in their sashes. The air was filled with golden leaves, luminous and bright against the leaden skies. They swirled through the air and fluttered at the upstairs windows like frightened birds, scratching at the panes.

By morning the lawns were a patchwork of fallen leaves, strewn with twigs and branches and saturated with rain. Our pond, once so low we considered building a small gangway for Ducky to reach dry land, was now brimming over uncontrollably. The springs that feed it were running so fast the drainage system could not cope with the overflow. Across the garden water poured out of the culverts turning the broad steps to the lower lawn into Niagara Falls and the lawn itself into a flooded paddy field. A group of stray cattle added to the mayhem by wandering freely on a tour of inspection, slipping and sliding down the slopes and munching their way through the herbaceous border.

The dogs love the storms. They are energised and excited by their power. I find them frightening and exhausting. I am beginning to feel like one of those wayward socks that get lost in the washing machine. Battered and threadbare. I've lost count of how many wash cycles we've been through but it seems like we've been stuck somewhere between Soak and Fast Spin for a very long time.

The rising floodwaters of the past month have coincided with a rising level of discontent amongst motorists, road-hauliers, farmers and pensioners creating, quite literally, a groundswell of misery for all concerned. With their fields waterlogged our farmers, already in desperate circumstances, now face the possibility of being unable to drill their winter crops. Sheep farmers are under threat of wholesale slaughter of their flocks to safeguard against BSE. Pig farmers are battling against the onslaught of disease. Families bravely try to salvage their homes and possessions from the floods and pensioners have to fight for what is right-fully theirs. Our politicians spin and launder the facts while the country frets and feels the chill. Throughout Britain there are people struggling to cope with the destruction of their lives. The storms have abated some-what after Mr. Brown's Canute-like defiance of the rising tide of demon-strations, but the rot has set in. When the floodwaters subside many Britons will find their foundations increasingly eroded and the familiar structures of their lives close to collapse.

Thankfully no rain today and a patch of blue sky above the tulip tree. It frames a pair of buzzards wheeling freely on the rising air and a flurry of gulls blown inland from the sea. The autumn colours are spectacular this year. Guy Fawkes would be proud of their display. Glorious canopies of gilded leaves explode like fireworks against the sky, fanning out into glit-tering arcs of gold and yellow, bronze and green. Briefly they hang suspended in time and space, shimmering fragments of autumn confetti, before flickering and falling finally to earth.

Small birds are clustering around the feeders, swinging gaily to and fro. Woodpeckers, tits and finches gather in the nearby shrubs to await their turn. Occasionally a magpie swoops down and scares them all away or a blue winged jay screeches from the oak tree above. Wild pheasant have joined the peafowl on the doorstep to eat their corn and a shy wren hides beneath the overhanging rose. Oh, the strangest thing has happened to Betty our remaining peahen. She is changing into a peacock! We can hardly believe our eyes! First her brown neck feathers turned white and we thought it was simply old age. Now they have turned bright blue like the males. Even more extraordinary, she is now growing a male tail! We can't understand it at all. What is happening?? It has certainly put us off eating peanuts. And, as a precaution, my husband now prefers to drink his whisky neat.

Life at Horswell is never dull! We have an unwelcome guest living with us at the moment. He or she has a very large appetite and a liking for Italian food. So far it has eaten two packets of Amaretti biscuits, a packet of bread sticks and a large hunk of Dolcelatte cheese.

It is very worrying. Yesterday I found my husband looking under the bed. He thinks I'm keeping a Latin lover!

I assured him he had nothing to fear and that I had heard loud scratching in the wall behind the kitchen dresser. Ratman was called. Alas, no evidence of the intruder's identity was found.

In the larder we now have a trap big enough to ensnare the 'beast of Bodmin'. It is baited with finest Italian chocolate and crumbled Amaretti biscuits. I am terrified to use the larder. Every day the size of the beast increases in my imagination. I'm expecting horns and cloven hooves at the very least.

So far nothing has happened. Our visitor is obviously intelligent as well as a connoisseur of fine food. I have a feeling that he is hoping to stay for Christmas. Knowing he is here, I wonder if our other guests will still want to join us?

It could provide the perfect excuse for having a quiet Christmas. Mmmm! I think I'm beginning to warm to him... Perhaps he could be persuaded to stay until the festivities are over? A little 'Vitello tonnato' on the menu tonight maybe?...

Happy Christmas!

24

January 2001

Repent ye sinners!

———◦◦◦◦———

We've tried it in every position, in the bedroom, the bathroom, even in the kitchen. We've even tried it holding our breath and balancing on one toe but STILL the scales point accusingly at an alarming increase in our body weight. Mince pies and Christmas pudding may have played their part but the growing heap of empty bottles seemed directly proportional to the increase in our girth. So suddenly, with our long awaited holiday looming, it was time to shake off hibernal sloth and tackle our seasonal 'avoir du poids'.

Eating lean healthy food is not difficult, indeed it provides a welcome respite from Christmas indulgence but having suffered an excess of water over the last months through both deluge and flood, to have to consume the wretched stuff as well seems particularly unfair. Especially as a bottle of wine is relatively easy to consume and, dare I say it, even pleasurable, whilst the daily two litres of mineral water prescribed for a healthy diet presents an almost unsurmountable challenge. It is, quite simply, too wet!

We had rather hoped that my husband's furtive night- time visits to the bottle bank might have gone unnoticed. After all, a rosy cheeked fellow with a false beard and a sack slung over his shoulder should hardly attract undue attention during the Christmas season. But alas we can only assume that our sinful forays have been exposed, for not one but three different religious groups have visited us in the last week offering to show us the folly of our ways and the path to salvation.

I had imagined that missionaries would be far too busy hacking their way through some Amazonian jungle to think of coming to Horswell; busy persuading devout tree-worshippers to become reluctant Christians. Or paddling up the Congo, hell bent on proving that the white man's medicine is superior to that of the local witchdoctor. I suppose with all the water rushing down our driveway recently they could be forgiven for thinking they had stumbled on some 'lost tributary of the Orinoco', but I am not too sure that they have signs saying 'Strictly Private' in the middle of a rainforest. Our sinful habits, it would appear, are not a 'Private' matter but up for grabs, with Seventh Day Adventists, Born Again Christians and Jehova's Witnesses battling for our souls.

Their leaflets spoke of damnation and redemption, preaching hope for the world to come and ringside seats for the followers of their particular church. A bit like a political party manifesto – 'Send your subscription and join us. We look after our own.' That is not for me. What I want to hear is that He will continue to exert the considerable forbearance and protection He has shown me in the past, and that the road to salvation is via Heathrow Airport and a holiday in Kenyan sunshine. After which the daffodils and camellias will be in full bloom, the tedium of gales and grey skies will be a distant memory and life in all its complexity will once again be a source of wonder and delight.

Nevertheless I admire their determination to battle through wind and rain to bring enlightenment to two sinners, three dogs and a transvestite peahen. Looking tired and oppressed by the burden of their mission they were unlikely to persuade me to join them. Whereas if a loose-limbed, bronze-skinned, re-born Aztec limboed into my life and tried to sell me the benefits of sun worship, he just might get a convert!

P.S. I think our resident rodent must have been late for a wedding. When we encountered him he was hurrying through the kitchen, resplendent in an outfit of morning-suit grey. From a distance it was hard to tell if he was Italian or not but the Mafia would have been proud of the speed and efficiency of his furry assassin. Bertie now styles himself Bertie 'the Rat'. We are hoping to be spared reprisals from the rest of the Mob.

25

MARCH 2001

Jambo! Habari?

———◆◉◆———

Jambo! Habari? Hello! How are you? Is winter over? Are the daffodils in bloom? Is it safe to come home?

I am writing from East Africa, on the Kenyan coast just south of Malindi. As I look out over the Indian Ocean the water is palest aquamarine streaked with violet and indigo, its deeps and shallows like dark veins and purple bruises beneath lustrous translucent skin. As far as the eye can see a broad curve of perfect white sand edges the ocean, separating it from a hinterland of coconut palms, the roofs of private residences just visible in their dense foliage. A varied fleet of sport fishing boats dots the horizon, their gleaming white hulls reflecting the sun and dazzling the eye. High prowed and low waisted they bristle with radar and radio masts, their rods splayed out on either side like insects' antennae.

At low tide the sea recedes to reveal an extensive coral reef pocketed with rock pools and large outcrops of coral of intricate shape. Idly we give them names. One, smoother than the others, low and long with an upturned tail becomes Whale Rock, another with angled holes like eyes pierced through it is Demon Rock, a third with a conical projection in the centre we call Smokestack.

Between the rocks small craft come and go collecting passengers and supplies from the beach to service the yachts anchored in the bay. The gentle putter of outboard engines is carried on the breeze mingling with the excited squeals of small children playing with their Aya in the shallows. Escorted by his owner a pale camel lurches and sways along the beach towards them adding to their delight.

As a smiling young waiter appears with a drink, ice tinkling in a frosted glass, it is hard to reconcile the luxury of this magical place with the backbreaking poverty and urban decay we have witnessed on our travels throughout the country. The former glories of Nairobi and Mombasa are lost now in a dusty haze of poverty and neglect, the romantic candle-lit stalls at night hiding the shabby squalour visible during the day.

Crumbling cratered roads have rattled our bones through scenes of immense beauty but also of such deprivation and human resourcefulness that their images remain seared into our consciousness. Lack of water and lack of investment in the country's infrastructure seem to be immense problems. Failed maize crops have left families with neither food nor income. Instead they take what they can from their parched land, digging for rocks and sand from the dry riverbed, carrying them in woven baskets to the roadside. Turbanned in rags against the blistering heat men sit cross- legged relentlessly hammering the larger rocks into building blocks, pounding the offcuts into loose road chippings and heaping them in piles beside the road in the hope of making a sale to a passing truck.

Brightly clad women trudge wearily beside the road balancing empty five gallon drums on their heads to the nearest watering hole, often several miles away. Later we see them struggling home laden like beasts of burden. A wide band around their foreheads supports the water now resting heavily on their backs. They clasp their hands behind their heads to prevent their necks snapping backwards with the weight. The water supply when we see it is often fetid or stagnant, a herd of cows trampling the muddy banks.

In towns simple roadside stalls lie dusty and disused through lack of produce. Where there are fruit or vegetables they are stacked three high at the front to disguise the emptiness of the tray behind. Another stall may boast a single hubcap or windscreen wiper blade gleaned from the roadside in the hope of making a sale. Wood carvers and metal workers ply their trade. Beside them braziers char the bark of mango trees for fuel. Old shoes, battered and misshapen from hard use are offered for sale along with second hand clothes. Between the stalls immaculate children with neatly braided hair play happily in the dust whilst men sit around unfed and unemployed returning dark stares to the tourists' waving hands.

The earth is rich and red like Devon soil, the prosperity or failure of its crops dependant upon a reliable and accessible water supply. Where water is available we drive through neat plantations of sisal, pineapples, peas, tea, coffee, roses and carnations. It is easy to see that governed and managed well the potential for Kenya is enormous. Already several Jumbo Jets leave Nairobi every day laden with green beans and roses for the UK, presumably to other countries too –and yet the country's vital services seem in terminal breakdown with power and water supplies, roads, transport, schools and hospitals in desperate need of investment and organisation. Some international aid agencies are now cutting back their aid programmes citing 'lack of transparency in the handling of their funds' as the reason. Sadly the problems seem unsurmountable.

In the countryside it is extraordinary how little the twentieth century has altered a way of life practised for generations. The houses are still made of mud, the men erecting a framework of thin wooden supports then leaving it to the women to fill in all the gaps with a mixture of mud and cow dung, rather like a bird building a nest. Nearer the coast the roofs are steeply pitched and covered with palm thatch, which allow a cooling passage of air within the house. Inland, where material for thatch is not available, the roofs are lower, rounded and made, like the walls, of mud. Some have galvanised tin roofs which withstand the Winter rains well but, without the appropriate insulation, in Summer heat the house to intolerable temperatures.

Polygamy enables the men to ensure a male heir, but also to leave their homes in search of work, sure in the knowledge that their land is being cared for by the women left behind. The more land he has, the more wives he needs to look after it. Traditionally the man has his own house, with separate houses for each wife. This is not as democratic as it first appears as the wives have to share their homes with not only their children but their goats too! Meanwhile Papa shares his with the food supplies and a gourd full of alcohol!

In the Mara, a vast area of grassland in the south of the country close to the border with Tanzania, the Maasai tend their herds of cows and goats as they have throughout history. Young boys awaiting circumcision, their rite of passage into adulthood, live with their animals away from their homes with just a blanket, a pointed stick, a club and a bow and arrow for protection from the wild animals that hunt and kill beside them on the Mara. Traditionally a Maasai could not be called a warrior until he had killed a lion with his bare hands. They survive on milk and blood and maize, and the camaraderie of their peers. They are tall and lean, darkly handsome in their brilliant red robes and multi-coloured beads, as exotic as all the birds and animals we had come to see.

We saw leopard, cheetah, lions with their cubs, hyena, gazelle, impala, oryx, wildebeest, dik-dik, waterbuck, buffalo, zebra, elephants, giraffe, rhino, crocodiles and hippopotami –to name but a few! And all at such close quarters we could have reached out and touched them –but then I suppose I wouldn't still be here to tell the tale! The birds and butter-flies alone were so numerous and beautiful they deserved a safari dedi-cated solely to them. We saw herons and storks, flamingos and ostrich, sea eagles and osprey, secretary birds and guinea fowl, kingfishers and weaver birds, pelicans and hornbill, many others too.

Here on the coast the sport fishers have returned with their catch. We sit having tea, like tricoteuses at the guillotine, as enormous Marlin, Sailfish and Shark are hoisted and weighed on the gallows, photographs taken and experiences shared. The sun slips down behind the palms leaving the sea pale and smooth as an opal, glinting with fire. Soon cock-tails will be served followed by Dinner under the stars. In the warm dark-ness of sudden night I reflect on our holiday. Memories are filed like snapshots in my head. All vivid and remarkable. A feast for the senses, to sustain us through grey English days to come.

Flicking quickly through my mental photo album I see huge croco-diles slithering out of muddy rivers, heaving their gross bodies up onto the mudflats to snap and crunch at bones left for them there; the shores of Lake Nkuru rimmed pink with thousands and thousands of wading flamingo, small flashes of yellow as weaver birds dart in and out of their nests which hang suspended like fruit from the thorn trees; three magnif-icent cheetahs singling out an impala from its herd and chasing it to its death; the leopard lying fat and sleek in a tree after eating a small gazelle; in a nearby clearing the gazelle's mother watching pitifully with mournful eyes; the cobalt blue and speckled black plumage of the vulturine guineafowl worthy of a creation by Dior; the ridiculous gait of an ostrich on the run, like a ballerina on points; the sight of an osprey soaring against a cloudless blue sky; a convention of enormous black and white storks like balding professors discussing the merits of standing on one leg; the size of the elephant that blocked our path trumpeting for us to get out of its way; the beauty of the giraffes galloping across the plains or standing tall amongst the trees plucking at leaves.

I remember our amusement at the hippos plodding about on the riverbed and coming up for air with a terrific whoosh and snorting and blowing of bubbles. Apparently they are vegetarians and will travel ten miles from water in search of food. I loved the big grey baboons following one another Indian style maybe thirty or forty of them at a time, the elders walking purposefully, setting the pace, the young ones tumbling off their mothers' backs to play and squabble with their peers, the babies tucked up close to their mothers' chests suckling her milk and peeping out with bush baby eyes.

Then there are the colours, the sounds and the smells: I see vibrant cascades of Bougainvilleia trailing through trees and over palmthatch –crimson, magenta, gold and white; fields of tall Sunflowers –splashes of sunshine yellow against red earth; brilliant blue Morning Glory winding through creepers; the pendulous bells of Datura –white against dark leaves; the flaming orange-red of Casuarina trees; the soft blue of Jacarandas made pale by the intensity of the sky. I hear the lions roaring in the still morning air and the chit chat of birds, the Mambo rhythm of African music and the soft spoken 'Hakuna matata' –'No worries' of the gentle Kenyan people. I am reminded of our driver's reply when I asked if we really should have driven over the Tanzanian border to see the leopard. 'We are not allowed', he said 'But the road is taking us'. I smell the dry musk of red earth, elephant and lion, the cloying sweetness of the waxy frangipani blooms and now, as I write, taste the saltiness of the sea.

As our last day in this earthly paradise draws to an end I turn my thoughts to Horswell, to Abo and Bertie and Flossie. I close my eyes and imagine them running to greet us. I try and hear them barking their greeting but all I can hear is the scrape of cicadas and the sound of the sea sighing in its sleep, the rise and fall of its breath muffled by a soft pillow of sand.

26

May 2001

A sad farewell

Not long ago we were railing against the cruelty, the ugliness of Nature. The fox killed our beloved Ducky, leaving only his feathers and a trail of blood to greet us instead of his usual quacking sprint across the lawn, orange feet going flippety-flap, often tripping him up in his haste. As if that were not harsh enough, our female mallard was disturbed from her nest where she had been sitting on eggs for the past month. The nest was destroyed and all her eggs had been taken. As she sat quietly mourning her loss, three wild mallard drakes, all intent on mating, jumped on her with such ferocity that we found her dead and bleeding from their attack.

Compared with the farmers who have had to cope with the horror of foot and mouth and the mass slaughter of their flocks and herds, I suppose we should not complain, but we were terribly sad to lose our plucky little friend and then, so soon afterwards, his family too. They gave us such pleasure, there seemed no justice in their demise.

Now, a week later, we are marvelling at Nature's beauty, the artistry of her compositions. Splashes of acrylic colour illuminate the garden; the pinks and reds of camellias, orange, mauve and yellow azaleas, rhodo-dendrons of purple and magenta. Broad brushstrokes against a clear blue sky. Meanwhile in the hedgerows bluebells, buttercups, campion and purple orchids have replaced the fading primroses, their vibrant colours speckled against lush green grass like drops of paint from an Impression-ist's brush.

Nature is a paradox, ugly and yet so beautiful. Perhaps it is necessary to have those two extremes to give us balance, to act as benchmarks between which we can find normality. Without hot how would we know cold, without ugliness how would we appreciate beauty, without misery how intensely would we feel joy? Above all it teaches us to value the present, in the knowledge that all things are ephemeral and likely to change. Especially the weather!

The sun has come out at last. Having been floundering for months in the darkness of rain storms and devastating disease, someone has finally found the switch and turned on the light. Summertime has arrived in a rush and now, with an election looming on the horizon, it is suddenly time to take stock of the world around us and consider our future.

Looking at the state of the country I find it rather like looking at the state of our garden. After the dismal start to the year things are not quite as rosy as one might have hoped. Illegal immigrants, like weeds, have taken root and spread, straining our resources. Traditional structures have been weakened by the winds of change and many well established English features are in the process of being uprooted and thrown on the rubbish heap. Although some new introductions from Europe have cross fertilised successfully, others are threatening our indigenous English species with their restrictive red-tape bindings. New ideas that showed so much early promise no longer appear to flourish and seeds, planted in hope four years ago, have either not materialised or have failed to come up to expectation.

Wordsworth once wrote 'I have learned to look on nature, not as in the hour of thoughtless youth; but hearing often-time the still sad music of humanity.' At this time of year both our gardens and our country need our attention.

After the long winter and endless rain it is tempting to ignore the hectic electioneering going on around us and simply enjoy the pleasures of early summer. The warmth of sunshine is beguiling, as is the sweet clean air laden with birdsong and the scent of blossom. At last we have the opportunity to tend our gardens or to entertain outdoors while bumble bees drone lazily around our heads. It would be easy for us to close our eyes and leave our politicians to do their work. But perhaps we should remember that 'Power corrupts and absolute power corrupts absolutely'. It is interesting that the word 'politic' when referred to in the Dictionary means 'artful or shrewd, crafty, unscrupulous or cunning' and that 'politicians' are persons 'actively engaged in politics'. Elections are not a time for apathy but a time to be alert and aware. As Thomas Paine (1737-1809) opined: 'Government, even in its best state is but a necessary evil; in its worst state, an intolerable one.'

One of the hardest things to accept is that for every person who is passionately 'for' one course of action, there is another for whom it is a complete anathema. Political differences and open discussion are an integral part of the freedom and tolerance we enjoy in this country, and so often take for granted. In the name of democracy, we agree to disagree. Tobias George Smollett (1721-1771) wrote 'I think for my part one half of the nation is mad and the other not very sound' which seems to ring as true today as it did then.

Elections are divisive times. They force us to decide on which side of the fence we want to sit; to create the two extremes like hot and cold, ugliness and beauty, left and right that ensure a fair debate and a moderate centre path. Perhaps more importantly they force us to look carefully at past achievements and future plans. To look beyond the propaganda and the clever sound bite, the pop stars and the photo opportunities and see for ourselves how and where our country is being led.

Leaders in France and Germany speak openly of a European Socialist state, a place where countries 'no longer exist, only Europe'. So if we integrate with Europe that means 'Farewell to England'. The government has promised if re-elected to 'change this country beyond all recognition' dividing it into self-governing regions, undermining the power of parliament in Westminster, the historic 'Mother of all Parliaments'. So it really will be 'Farewell to England'.

I prefer to view Europe as a friendly neighbour. To use the garden analogy again, I enjoy looking at my neighbours' gardens. They are different from our own. Some are bigger, some smaller, some more colourful, some more beautiful, some more organised and some in disarray. It gives me pleasure to see them. I delight in their endless variety and am happy to learn from their success. I enjoy sharing information, trading ideas and plants, even visiting them occasionally, but despite our cordial relationship I do not feel either the desire or the necessity to take down the walls and hedges that divide us. I do not expect to subsidise their failures when a repayable loan could be available and if they started interfering in my garden and telling me what to do I would not be amused! Neither, I suspect, would they!

I know that there are many people who are eager for England to submit to the power of the European Super State. The cross on my ballot paper will do little to dissuade them. They are entitled to their view and I to mine. Thankfully we live in a democracy, for the present at least. But the thought of becoming a 'region' of Europe under a centralised government in Brussels fills me with dread. I cannot help endorsing the words of Charles Churchill (1731-1764), in his poem appropriately called 'The Farewell': 'Be England what she will, with all her faults, she is my country still'.

England is our garden, our own backyard, our home, our way of life, our future. It has given us peace, stability, respect, a thriving economy and a tolerant society. It has been a place of refuge for the persecuted and a beacon of justice and integrity. It has been our protector and our friend and yet we are preparing to throw it with a hop skip and a jump into the European pond to sink without trace.

As Thomas Paine said: 'These are times that try men's souls'.

He also said: 'My country is the world and my religion is to do good'.

If only our modern politicians would accept his words as their creed.

27

JULY 2001

Bon Voyage! Bon Retour!

━━━━◆◉◉◉◆━━━━

We had no sooner decided to escape the doom and gloom of pre-election England than summer arrived and bathed the country in glorious sunshine making us wonder why we were leaving. But, with housesitters arranged, we headed South, taking the inaugural flight with 'Go' airlines from Bristol to Nice. Champagne flowed and a carnival atmosphere prevailed, with stilt walkers, jugglers, fire eaters and clowns to entertain us and wish us 'Bon voyage'. An hour and a half later we arrived in the South of France, thankfully every bit as sunny as England and considerably hotter, and picked up our hire car. Soon we were cruising along the Promenade des Anglais in a snazzy black convertible, heading for lunch in the old port of Villefranche.

One of the things I like most about the French Riviera is how little it changes. I love the architecture, the impatient traffic, the pace, the congestion, the style. Happily all the archetypes are still there:

● The dapper old man in cream jacket and cravat, walking an aged miniature poodle on a lead from 'Hermes'.

- The wrinkled old lady, heavily rouged and immaculately coiffed, clutching the latest 'Gucci' handbag in a red taloned claw.

- The pretty young girls riding pillion on scooters that burp and whine recklessly through the traffic.

- The dashing young man in the open Porsche, who eyes the girls then checks his own appearance in the rearview mirror, smiling at what he sees.

- The lime-washed buildings in ice cream colours; pistachio, lime, citron and melon, honey and butterscotch, peaches and cream.

- Geraniums spilling from ironwork balconies.

- Tall shuttered windows enfolding the secrets of cool dark interiors.

- The whiff of intrigue and forbidden romance.

And all the theatre of it played out against a backdrop of the bluest sea and the largest, most magnificent yachts imaginable.

From Villefranche to the glorious mansions of Cap Ferrat, then on to Monaco to crawl gridlocked around the Grand Prix circuit to see the preparations for the race the following day. From there, inland to the sun drenched villages of the Alps Maritimes, the Luberon and Vaucluse for two weeks of good food and sensational scenery, enchanting architecture and fascinating discoveries. I shall never again be able to smell the scent of lavender without conjuring in my mind's eye the acres of lavender grown in the Luberon. With snow capped mountains in the distance etched against a sharp blue sky, field upon field of mauvey blue stripes create a herringbone weave over rolling foothills as far as the eye can see. At the end of July when it is fully in flower the scent will fill the air, attracting swarms of honey bees and tourists too. Beside the neat rows of lavender, sunflowers are grown for seed and oil, their brilliant yellow vibrant against the lavender blue.

With cherry orchards, almonds, olives and vines the scenery changes dramatically with the seasons and offers sumptuous produce for the market stalls. Markets in Provence are a feast for all the senses. Brightly woven baskets, local pottery and Provencal fabrics jostle for space with lavender bags, lavender oils, lavender wax, homemade soaps, olive oils, beeswax candles, jars of honey, sacks of herbs, local jams, sugared fruits, toasted almonds, bars of nougat, not to mention the infinite variety of flowers and plants, vegetables, cheeses, meat and fish.

We returned from Provence intoxicated by the sights and smells, enriched by the colours and the light that have inspired so many artists to capture them on canvas. It was hard to leave it all behind. We wondered if our home coming would seem drab and dull in comparison. But the Horswell ghosts always know when they are on trial. They know our moods too well to risk disappointing us. And sure enough, as we turned up the drive and looked out across the lawn, they had ensured that the house and garden had never looked more beautiful. They seemed to be reaching out to us with their most seductive smile, eager to enfold us in a warm embrace. We agreed it was, after all, good to be home and could feel a collective sigh of relief whisper around us.

As I sit outside and write Betty, our transvestite peahen, dozes under my chair. Her soft feathers are blown by the wind and tickle my feet. Nearby the two peacocks, Imran and Genghis, lie peacefully together, thoughts of mating and rivalry now forgotten. Their immensely long tails are folded neatly behind them, gleaming in the sun light, tipped with swirls of sapphire and emerald, edged with gold. They are quieter now as they enter their moulting season, gradually discarding feathers one by one. Like the dogs, they enjoy companionship, content to be near us and soak up the warmth of the sun. Beside me Abo, our adored old Labrador, sleeps deeply under the cherry tree, his handsome head cushioned on silver paws. Flossie the sheepdog is busy in the orchard helping her master to rake up hay. Bertie meanwhile, ever a law unto himself, is taking a Jacuzzi in the fountain! Half submerged, he walks round and around the pond under the sparkling cascade of water, cooling his fur. Having ensured he now has my full attention, he leaps out of the water and zigzags across the lawn in a mad dog run, showering a haze of crystal droplets into the air around him.

We have been privileged this year to be visited for the first time by a pair of swallows. They made their nest on a ledge in the old tack room. Having successfully raised their young they are now busy teaching them to fly. How we love to see them with their long black tails and swooping flight, slicing through the air on invisible curves. They fly so close we could reach out and touch them. Then they bank sharply and wheel high into the sky, dark wings flickering against the cloudless blue. They circle overhead in joyous spirals calling to one another 'tswee, tswee'. Then, with a final triumphant lap of the courtyard, they stream back to their nest with the speed and precision of a flight of arrows hitting their mark. Could they, I wonder, be from the family of swallows that dive-bombed us in Kenya as we sat outside our safari lodge writing postcards home? At the time we thought we might be sitting too close to their nest. Now I think they may have been trying to look over our shoulders to memorise our postal address!

I have often wondered why birds migrate from Africa to England. Surely our summers can barely be much warmer than African winters? But like our trip to Kenya and our recent visit to France, maybe it is only by seasonal migration that one fully appreciates the pleasures of being at home.

28

SEPTEMBER 2001

I love September…

———◈◈◈———

I love September. It's a high altitude plateau between Summer and Autumn. A place where one can pause to take stock and admire the view. Look back and one can relive the pleasures of the Summer. Look forward and we can prepare for the new season that lies ahead. As the last car door slams after the last tearful goodbye and the grandchildren disappear down the drive in a flurry of waving hands it is with mixed feelings that we realise that the holidays are over.

The children leave looking brown and fit, wearing their new surfer tee shirts and clutching their beach-combed treasures. They enquire anxiously about the safety of the pottery they have hand painted in Totnes and the whereabouts of the small stuffed elephant so disastrously forgotten on a previous visit. Exhausted, we stand on the step and wave our goodbyes. We are left with our ears still ringing and a house strangely still, but also with the warmth of their love, an assortment of their artworks and a wealth of unforgettable memories.

The terrace where we dine by candlelight provides a natural stage for those with theatrical leanings. There we have been entertained with handstands and cartwheels, virtuoso performances from the latest school play and the basso voce solos of newly broken voices. On the beach young sharp eyes turned our attention to luminous pebbles that gleamed like agates amongst the oatmeal tweed of granular sand; to the pretty white shell and the small rounded fragment of worn green glass. Each, a new and wondrous discovery, that without reminder we may have taken for granted. Back home for tea, the daily procession to Grandad's Bench is a memory I hope we will never forget.

Grandad's Bench, a Birthday present from the children earlier this year, is sited in the far paddock where it commands an outstanding view. In one direction is the tower of South Milton church, and across the valley outlined against the green hills, that of Thurlestone. Being far enough from the house to warrant a reasonable walk, the new seat has made it a favourite place to stop and rest awhile, an ideal spot for a picnic tea.

And so to the procession: First is Bertie, our big hairy dog proudly leading the way, barking importantly to frighten the rabbits and announce our arrival. Then comes Grandad wearing the idiotic hat of the day, driving his red tractor-mower. Behind the tractor he tows its small trailer containing a collection of the youngest grandchildren and their mother, all squealing with laughter and alarm in equal measure. Flossie the sheepdog is next, rushing around and around in chaotic circles, barking furiously at her unruly flock. In desperation she snaps at the tractor wheels and yelps with uncontrollable excitement. The rest of us follow on, bearing blankets and baskets, ready to push when the trailer gets stuck on the slippery slopes. Behind us comes the best sight of all, Old Abo our much loved and threadbare Labrador, reclining on a tartan blanket in the wheelbarrow as he is pushed with some difficulty uphill by our long-suffering and kind-hearted son in law. As we progress ceremoni-ously along the narrow woodland paths Abo peers nonchanantly over the barrow's edge, waving a regal paw. Attracted by all our laughter and hullabaloo Imran and Betty, two of the peafowl complete our retinue, pecking at the greenery and eyeing us in ever increasing disbelief.

But now that all our visitors have gone, there is lots to do. In the garden, ever keen to take advantage of our neglect, nature has been step-ping up the battle to regain its territory. Flowerbeds have become tangled and overgrown while roses amaze us with their profusion of second blooms. Hydrangeas and camellias wilt from lack of rain and hanging baskets beg for water. The lawns are parched and undermined by voles, their excavations now so extensive they rival the London Underground.

Tawny owls swoop and hoot through the trees and badgers root up the grass in search of leatherjackets. Squirrels are darting from tree to tree, stripping bark and stealing nuts. They sit in the plum trees eating fruit we cannot reach and drop the conkers from the chestnut trees to burst them from their spiney shells. Autumn cyclamen make welcome colour beneath the trees as high above them a pair of buzzards soar against a cloudless sky.

The new waterfall we have created is looking good. It will take a while for the stone to mellow and for the small ferns pushed into cracks to take root and grow, but the sound of water tumbling into the pond is very pleasing. We are eagerly assembling waterside plants to grow around it, with Gunnera, Rheums and Zantedeschia already in position. But first there is a lot of clearing and preparation to do around the whole area. Michael's elbow crutch is proving very useful for feeling the way across to the island. By using it to locate the building blocks we placed underwater at the shallowest point we can just manage to make the crossing without our waders filling with water. Even with it, crossing is a perilous business as the pondweed is dense and slimey and on either side of our makeshift causeway the water drops to 10 feet deep.

Yesterday, after a hard few hours clearing brambles and detritus from the island and having negotiated the causeway several times to assemble relevant tools and remove the considerable heap of clippings and rubbish I had accumulated, I had barely the energy to return to the house. Determined to get all my paraphernalia home in one go I tied the bucket around my neck and used it as a container for all my hand tools, gripped the crutch and rake in one hand, the spade and fork in the other then shuffled across the lawn as best I could with a back that was too stiff to hold upright and a pair of thigh waders that were four sizes too big.

Imagine, will you, my lack of enthusiasm when I was greeted by a husband too weak with laughter to speak coherently. When finally he managed to stammer a few words of greeting it was to tell me that I reminded him of Napoleon's retreat from Moscow. If I had had the energy I would have told him that I had not realised that he was old enough to know.

Through all of this our lovely house has looked like a ship in dry dock undergoing a refit. It is shrouded in scaffolding from top to toe with builders, carpenters and decorators crawling all over it as if playing a giant game of snakes and ladders. On the basis of 'If you're going to have a face lift you might as well have any other little flaws sorted out at the same time' repainting the house has developed into a complete overhaul of seemingly unlimited duration. It is like living inside an Advent calendar during the run up to Christmas, wondering which face will appear at which window, and, more importantly, when?

There seems to be no end in sight. In fact I'm now beginning to wonder how Christmas lights will look hanging off the scaffold. Better than the decorator?

29

CHRISTMAS 2001

After 9/11

———◆◈◆———

It is hard for us to comprehend the scale and effect of the destruction in New York, and the speed with which the aftershocks rippled out across the world to shake the familiar infrastructure of our lives and threaten our sense of security. At a stroke the terrorists have upped the stakes to unimaginable heights, going for broke in their bid to win this deadliest of games. We their opponents gasp in horror at their daring while our leaders evaluate the hand they've been dealt, shuffling and reshuffling events to ensure a commensurate response. Even our most experienced and hardened players must tremble as they play their cards and gamble with our lives.

In the wake of September 11th it was tempting to stay at home, in close contact with friends and loved ones, seeking reassurance that life, as we know it, had not been changed forever. But life, miraculously, goes on, outwardly much the same as before although, I suspect, more thoughtfully and with more awareness and appreciation of the fragile world around us. And so, despite a natural instinct to stay away, we settled into our familiar groove on the motorway and headed to London to keep appointments planned before that dreadful day when the whole world stood still.

Before lunch in the Butcher's Hall, we attended Harvest Festival in St. Bartholomew the Great's church in the heart of Smithfield. At the ceremony the Princess Royal was installed as the new Master of the Worshipful Company of Farmers. During her year in office she will provide a high profile for our struggling Agricultural industry, speaking out forcefully on the many issues that concern us.

At a later Harvest Thanksgiving service in St. Martin's in the Fields our boisterous rendition of 'We plough the fields and scatter' seemed strangely like a lament for a lost way of life, and totally in-congruous as we stepped out into the swirling traffic of Trafalgar Square. Black taxi cabs and double decker buses seemed about as far removed from ploughed fields as Mrs. Becket and her colleagues in DEFRA are from understanding the plight of those working in the countryside.

In golden sunshine we walked along the south embankment, past the London Eye, the Festival Hall and the wobbly Millennium Footbridge to the Tate Modern at Bankside for their Surrealist Exhibition. The much vaunted architecture of the great Turbine Hall (Empty) and the claustro-phobic exhibition galleries (Packed) failed to inspire us, but the views overlooking the river are superb. From there we walked to the Globe theatre and on to Southwark Cathedral where we sat peacefully with sunlight streaming through the tall windows. Prayers are said from the pulpit on the hour every hour, a heart-warming reminder that this is not a tourist attraction but a place of worship. By now a little footsore, we taxied back to the Royal Academy for lunch and an exhibition of 'Rembrandt's Ladies'. Thankfully their anatomy was less alarming than the ladies depicted at the Tate!

We saw two plays which underlined man's hypocrisy, the lengths to which he will go in his search for power and fame. One, 'Feelgood' at the Garrick pokes fun at the government's spin-doctoring whilst exposing its sinister manipulation of undesirable facts. The other, 'Mahler's Conversion' shows how Mahler denies his Jewish ancestry and converts to Catholicism in order to be accepted to conduct the Vienna State Orchestra. Unlike the politicians in 'Feelgood' who showed not the slightest remorse for their actions, Anthony Sher as Mahler conveys the inner turmoil of a man of conscience haunted by the denial of his true faith.

The State Rooms at Buckingham Palace, where we were invited to a cocktail party, provide an impressive cohesion of art and architecture. At night, softened by a candlelight glow, colours and gilding that might appear garish by day are subdued into an awesome opulence. Looking radiant in teal blue silk, the Princess Royal welcomes us to her home. Appearing relaxed and friendly she speaks to each of us in turn, remembering our names and interests with professional ease. I savour the moment, the burr of conversation, the liveried footmen, the tapestries and paintings that hang on silk covered walls, the ceilings exquisitely moulded and encrusted with gold leaf, the charm of our hostess. I shudder to think that in a different life I could be living in the dust bowl that is Afghanistan, without rights, without respect, without food; living a life so harsh, so devoid of expression and joy that one's spirit would be crushed almost to extinction.

Dogs and ducks and peafowl are there to greet us as we return to Horswell. Mmm! how sweet that salt laden air tastes as we ease our aching limbs out of the car and stretch away the tensions of a tedious journey. The house, bathed in autumn sunshine, seems strangely quiet. Then we realise the decorators have finished and the scaffolding has gone. Suddenly it is good to be home.

The fireworks this year made us feel uneasy. Not just because Bertie our gun-shy Briard trembles and shivers, yelping with fright until we let him share our bed and hug him tight (No greater love hath any dog owner!), but because every explosion sounds like a bomb, every bang like a gunshot that reminds us our country is at war. Whilst we gaze up at the heavens to admire the beautiful starbursts falling out of the sky there are people in Afghanistan looking up at B52 bombers and the projectiles that rain down upon them, intent on death.

Soon it will be Christmas, although the mild weather makes snow-capped chimneys and tinkling sleigh-bells harder than usual to imagine. Recent events will surely add an extra poignancy to what for many is already a bitter-sweet time of year. Hopefully amongst our introspection and concern for the future we will find time to simply relax and be merry, to enjoy our families and friends, to celebrate the many blessings of life and to offer a prayer for peace and goodwill to all men.

Happy Christmas!

30

JANUARY 2002

Taking down the Christmas decorations

―――――◦◦◦◦◦――――――

Taking down the Christmas decorations and returning them to their boxes for another year is a time of mixed emotions. On the one hand it is a time of new beginnings, of clearing the decks for a fresh new start, getting organised for what may lie ahead. But on the other, it seems that Christmas has come and gone all too quickly with little opportunity to reflect on the meaning and special beauty of this time of year.

As I carefully wrap each crystal droplet or golden ball, sparkling reindeer or twinkling star I enjoy looking back over Christmasses past; each ornament reminding me of its origin and unique history. All have been selected with infinite care, the few new ones each year adding to a collection which, over many years, has developed its own special character, its own special magic. Carrying the neatly packed boxes back down to the cellar I am aware that there is a small part of our lives captured forever in each of them. A snapshot of our hopes and dreams, our friends and family, our Christmas celebrations; a lifetime's memories wrapped in each and every one of those small pieces of tissue paper.

The garden at this time of year follows a similar pattern. Its special treasures, like the decorations in the cellar, have lain dormant all year waiting to delight us with their fragile beauty. Like the tree decorations, *individually* the plants are much the same, with only a few new additions. But as a *collection* their arrangement varies from year to year, never failing to excite us. Already we have early camellias, snowdrops and primroses, with the first aconite just appearing through the carpet of autumn leaves. As if to confirm that Spring will soon be on its way, this morning our white duck escorted four tiny yellow ducklings from her hut to the water's edge. Amongst much encouragement and congratulatory quacking from the other ducks and drakes they slipped into the cold water and swam serenely across the pond following in their mother's wake. We left them hiding beneath an overhanging leaf, anxiously watching the baby-snatching magpies and crows that materialised from out of nowhere.

Spotted woodpeckers are already drilling in the woods, coming to the feeders early in the morning, momentarily scaring the other birds away. A handsome cock pheasant in his golden tweed suit, white collar and black tie joins the peafowl on the step for breakfast peanuts, his plumage rivalling theirs in its intricate beauty. He looks remarkably small and vulnerable as the peafowl tower above him, magnificent in their new feathers, confident and proud. They play hide and seek with us around the glazing bars of the French Doors. Like small children they hide their eyes from us in the belief that if they can't see us then we can't see them. Not wanting to disappoint them, we play their game and look away as they pop their heads round the bars and peer in at us, then watch them quickly 'hide' as we look up and catch their eye. With their new tails growing fast, mating is already on their minds. Whereas all three have been happy to cohabit in the cork tree until now, Genghis, the weaker male, has already been despatched to solitary confinement in the Holm oak and is forced to eat alone. This seems particularly unfair as for the second year running Betty has come out of moult in full male plumage making her continuing interest in Imran a cause for speculation.

Traditionally this is the time of year for pantomimes and children's ballets. A time when little girls aspire to become, for an afternoon, Cinderella, the Sleeping Beauty or the Sugar Plum Fairy, encouraged by indulgent grandparents. It almost seems appropriate therefore that our country's 'Principal Boy', in a variety of fancy dress, should be strutting the boards of the world stage, expressing enough wishes for world peace to exhaust even the most generous Fairy Godmother.

Whilst we sit back and accept the usual suspension of disbelief associated with the entertainment industry Our Leader has become a card-carrying thespian. With professional ease and well-rehearsed emotions he dispenses largesse and bonhomie like stardust from a magic wand. Meanwhile, in the wings, the rest of the cast hover nervously, changing the scenery and trying not to lose their place in the script.

Dazzled by the spotlights our leader has recently embarked on a punishing tour. Undaunted by the many changes of role and costume required he has moved seamlessly from one theatre of war to another. Encouraged by good revues of his performance in flushing Ali Baba and the forty thieves from the Tora Bora mountains and recent appearances in India and Pakistan as the principal in The Emperor's New Clothes, he somewhat reluctantly accepted a minor role in the Zimbabwean smash hit Robin Hood before returning to the commons for a brief appearance in the ultimate pantomime: Prime Minister's Question Time.

As our Prime Minister aspires to be centre of the world stage, here in the Britain he has left behind, transport and postal workers are on strike, city workers spend more time gambling on train times than on stock markets, and farmers and fishermen stagger under increased legislation from Brussels. At the same time hospital waiting lists, crime and euro-scepticism continue to increase.

Our leader should be wary of turning a blind eye. With the benefit of a less exalted viewpoint a pantomime audience has the advantage. It can spot an approaching villain quicker than most: 'Behind you! Look behind you Mr. Blair! Behind you!'

Our 'Principal Boy' would do well to heed our heartfelt cries.

31

MARCH 2002

G'day! From the far side of the world

———⊷◦◦◦⊷———

G'day! from the far side of the world. I am visiting my father in Queensland, Australia where I had hoped, at least for a while, to avoid the English weather and the dreary politics. And what do I find? That after a summer of record temperatures there is now ' a monsoon trough over the Queensland coast and a high in the South China Sea' which is an exotic way of saying that it's raining and blowing a gale. Then, I discover that Mr. Blair has followed me out here and is just down the road at Coolum at the Commonwealth Conference! Is there no escape??

Hervey Bay where my father lives is a low-lying sandy stretch of coastline sheltered by Fraser Island, the largest sand island in the world; a World Heritage site famous for its scenic beauty and abundant wildlife. Between August and October it is host to migrating Humpback whales. To the delight of visitors and residents the whales return each year to enjoy the warm shallow waters. Here they rest and play, schooling their young calves in preparation for their forthcoming journey to the feeding grounds off the Antarctic coast. The wide beaches and balmy climate make Hervey Bay a delightful, easy-going place to live with the emphasis on a healthy outdoor lifestyle.

Between rainstorms the sea and sky are a vivid blue and the temperature hovers around 30C. The days here have a different structure from those at home, commencing early to avoid the heat of the day. Not known for my early morning starts, I am struggling to adjust my personal clock! Take this morning for example:

A ceiling fan is batting the air above my bed. The thin sheet covering my body feels hot and heavy as a duvet. I am woken by the constant flow of conversation from the balcony next to mine. I hear the words:

'Three down', 'Four across' and 'A word with seven letters, beginning with a P.'

Fully awake now, I get up and check my watch, wondering if I have overslept. It is 4a.m., pitch black and stiflingly hot. The light next door outlines an elderly couple sitting, fully dressed, on their balcony, deeply engrossed in a crossword puzzle. I climb back into bed and try to go to sleep, pulling the sheet up over my ears. But still I can hear them, their voices growing louder with every new success. The clues are mind numbingly simple even at this early hour and my brain screams with frustration at their slow, halting progress. Again and again they return to the seven-letter word beginning with P:

'Look Ma, if twelve down is correct it must begin with a P and end with an L'

Unable to stop myself I scan my mental dictionary and decide on the word 'Parasol'. I long to tell them and put an end to their agonising (and their noise!) Trying to ignore their tiresome guesswork I listen to the rhythmic beat of the ceiling fan and let my mind wander over the past few days:

A Buddhist I met in a Singapore coffee shop suggested I visit two places, Maleny and Montville. Our meeting had been so brief and unexpected it seemed like a message from the gods so on leaving Brisbane they were my first port of call. He was right. They were beautiful. Small, arty, stylish towns set in the verdant grandeur of the Glass House Mountains. I remember their lush rainforests and the whisps of raincloud floating like ghosts in the valleys below.

'It's got an R in it Ma! Look. P something – R something – Something, something – then L.'

I try to blot out the intrusion with thoughts of the beautiful beach below me. I picture the huge acreage of golden sand that is revealed by the falling tide. I see the sinuous ribbons of sky-reflecting water that snake between newly exposed sand flats to create a constantly changing landscape of low smooth islands and shallow lagoons. I recall the sight of a sea eagle perched on a wooden post, the breeze ruffling his feathers. Motionless, he concentrates on the pool below. Suddenly he swoops down into the water, emerging with a sizeable fish which he carries off, suspended like a missile, beneath him.

The puzzlers are getting louder, putting an end to all hopes of sleep:

'It's got an S in it too Ma. Look, I've just done ten down.'

'What was that dear?'

'Possum'

'Oh, well done dear. 'Possum'. That was a hard one.'

I listen to the sound of the rolling surf and remember how the breeze sends shivers across the smooth blue water in the bay, making the surface shimmer and dazzle with reflected light.

'What was that clue again dear?'

I take a deep breath to calm my irritation, soothing my mind with thoughts of the grey heron that stands on one leg beside the swimming pool, and the white ibis that peck at grubs in the sand with their long black beaks. In my mind I can see vibrant orange dragonflies that dance in the blue air on whirring wings. I see the black swallows that dive and flicker past my window and listen to the echo of the butcher bird's melodic, bell-like song.

'Here we are Ma. P something – R something – S something – L. Seven letters. 'For too much sun'.'

I hold my breath, awaiting her reply.

'Could that be 'suncream' dear?'

I stifle my groan by biting the sheet.

'Strewth Ma, this is a hard one!'

I ball my fists tightly, close my eyes and visualize walking along the beach. I see the long wooden jetty reaching out into the sea and feel the hard ribbed sand wet beneath my feet. I walk nearer the foreshore where the sand is soft and warm between my toes. Beside me gum trees, wattle, tamarisk and myrtle tangle in natural profusion. A flock of green-backed parrots cling and sway on the branches of the overhanging casuarina trees. Raucously they squabble over their black spikey fruits. Suddenly afraid, they take to the air with an ear splitting screech, their rainbow colours vibrant against the sky.

'*I've got it Ma!*' the puzzler yells with startling enthusiasm.

'Got what *dearie?*'

'*Parasol!*' he shouts. It's Parasol!

My body relaxes, limp with relief. I listen to their guffaws of self congratulation and check my watch. It is 5.30 a.m. Pink streaks have appeared in a pale grey sky and the air fills with the birds' joyful chorus. I get up and take a cup of coffee out onto the balcony. The first rays of golden sunshine warm my skin and the air smells fresh and clean. Pale shadows sculpt the beach into sensuous curves as gentle waves unfold on the unmarked sand. A man in a red checked shirt splashes along the waterline, his Blue-Heeler cattle dog running beside him. They disturb a flock of gulls. Then a large grey heron flaps slowly into the thin morning air.

I look across at the puzzlers' balcony and see they have retreated indoors. Although I am grateful that they have disappeared, inwardly I thank them for introducing me to this most perfect hour of the day.

P. S. The telephone rings, shattering my new-found peace. A call from home. Sad, sad news; I have lost my dearest friend. Abo, our beloved Labrador has passed away.

32

May 2002

Return to Cuckoo Land

———◆◈◆———

Citizens, relax in the knowledge that Britain's shores are, contrary to all reports, fiercely guarded against unwanted asylum seekers. Believe me, I know from personal experience. On my return from Australia I was grilled for over half an hour by Immigration, threatened with deportation and accused of being an illegal immigrant. Apparently a vital stamp had been omitted from my new passport.

Only intense negotiation prevented me from having to return to Australia and submit my 'case for entry into Britain' to the Home Office. Had it actually come to that, I most assuredly would not have bothered to return. Not only was the situation galling after a 24 hour flight, but also patently absurd. As I stood at the Immigration desk, the epitome of Englishness in my Marks and Sparks cardigan, plane loads of Arabs, Asians and Orientals, many of whom spoke not one word of English, passed ahead of me without demur, waving shiny new British passports at disinterested officials.

It seems to me we are living in a crazy world. Like Alice, I sometimes feel as if I've fallen down a rabbit hole into a country where nothing makes sense:

- A country where a mother is jailed for 60 days because her children play truant from school and yet the law allows known paedophiles to live freely within the community.

- A country where a footballer earns £9.5 million a year and an old lady is beaten to death for the humble supper she has purchased from the local fish and chip shop.

- A country where so much is wrong and nobody is accountable, where politicians are paid for talking rather than achieving, where ordinary people pay higher and higher taxes for public services whose standards sink lower and lower.

- A country where our public transport system is in crisis; a system that is so desperately under-funded, unreliable and unsafe that its policies are examined not by a capable Minister for Transport, or even the Prime Minister himself, but in discussions held with the Prime minister's wife!

Whatever next? In comparison, Mad Hatters and croquet with flamingos sounds entirely sane.

Perhaps the confusion is something to do with the extraordinary conjunction of planets grouping together on our western horizon. For the first time in many years the elliptical orbits of Mars, Venus, Saturn, Jupiter and Mercury have brought them close enough to earth to be seen shining clearly in the night sky.

As they gather under the sign of Gemini, astrologers tell us that the influence of these heavyweight opponents will create turmoil in our lives. Those of us born under the sign of the Twins are supposed to be under the greatest pressure. For us, it is the celestial equivalent of having Ariel Sharon, Yassir Arafat, our husband, our lover and a long-lost relative all staying in our house at the same time! Stressful! Thankfully soon they will be on their way, out of sight and out of mind, allowing some normality to return to our lives.

Thank goodness for the sanctuary of Horswell House – a world at peace, a world I love and understand. Here, ducks sit huddled on their clutch of eggs or nurture ducklings under their wing. Seagulls and Jackdaws make unlikely bedfellows, nesting side by side on the roof-top. Ravens keep watch from a nearby treetop perch, deriding their neighbourly squabbles with a dry rattling laugh. Everywhere small song-birds flit to and fro feeding their young in hidden nests. The peafowl are full of noise and bluster, each parading a magnificent fan of feathers and hurling profanity at the black rainclouds of approaching storms.

The woods are filled with bluebells, pushing up through untidy clumps of overgrown primrose leaves. Their hyacinth scent fills the air and attracts the hum of bees. On bare twigs new leaves appear, fragile as emerging butterflies. Tentatively, they spread their pale green wings and flutter gently in the dappled sunshine. On mossy banks the lime green fronds of nascent ferns stand tall, unwinding from the tight spring of their Winter coils. Beside them garlic, white and pungent, makes foaming lace around the slender stems of stinging nettle, dock, and pink flowered campion.

In the garden the box hedges are neatly trimmed but growing still, with lavender and roses starting to bloom and scent the air. Glorious days have enabled us to eat our meals outside at last, providing an opportunity to savour the warmth of the sun and the luscious beauty of this our private world. I am reminded of Thomas Hardy's famous poem:

'This is the weather the cuckoo likes,
And so do I;
When showers betumble the chestnut spikes. And nestlings fly.
And the little brown nightingale bills his best,
And they sit outside at 'The Travellers Rest',
And maids come forth, sprig-muslin dressed,
And citizens dream of the south and west,
And so do I.'

33

July 2002

Raising the standard!

———◦◦◦◦◦———

President Bush and Mr. Blair have made me feel uneasy with their rattling sabres and threats of pro-active air strikes on Iraq. Add to that, the flagrant deception of global corporations, the helter-skelter slide of the world's stock markets and the subsequent lowering of our personal gold reserves and I'm ready to make a stand. It is time for the parting of our ways! After much consideration I have decided to follow in the footsteps of Rhodesia's Ian Smith by declaring Unilateral Independence for Horswell, thus freeing myself and those of like mind (Birds, ducks etc. if you're wondering!) from the reckless stupidity of our leaders. As of today, Horswell is now declared an independent nation state.

The country that we have left behind, once recognisable as England but now akin to Animal Farm, will surely soon be labelled 'Orwellia' in deference to the author and architect of its present incarnation. I therefore propose that my new country be called, by way of antithesis, 'Horswellia'.

Lack of Ministers or means of proper parliamentary debate will not be a problem. After all, we know don't we, that a country can be run easily by only two people and a handful of cronies, closeted together over a cup of coffee? Why bother with opposition when you can make all the rules yourself ? My husband fits perfectly into the role of Chancellor of the Exchequer, and as the one with the penchant for foreign holidays and the airy-fairy ideas on how to save the world, the role of Prime Minister will obviously fall to me.

Security seems to be one of the priorities of any newly free country. Bertie, the Briard, can be our Minister of Defence, and will be mostly occupied with border patrols and retrieving missiles, while Flossie the sheepdog is a natural for Home Secretary. Having initially snapped angrily at their heels, she will quickly roll over on her back and shower all asylum seekers with tokens of her affection.

Even for Horswellia, illegal immigrants could pose a considerable problem. Squirrels are multiplying fast, slugs are devouring our native flora, and rabbits are slipping through our defences as easily as a swarm of Eastern Europeans escaping from Sangatte. Despite Bertie's best efforts to catch them, the rabbits always outwit him, disappearing down their burrows quicker than a refugee escaping through the Channel Tunnel.

Like all independent nations, balancing the economy, is a critical part of our survival. Monthly negotiations of all expenditure and trade agreements will enable the Iron Chancellor to keep a grip on Horswellian affairs, despite his Prime Minister's far-flung largesse and continuing desire to 'make a difference' in people's lives.

Sadly these days there is a considerable trade deficit, with imports far exceeding exports. As Prime Minister I blame it on the strong pound and the poor exchange rate. The Chancellor calls it 'a lack of the work ethic' or 'creative accounting'. Either way, we realise, as a small country, our service industries are our strength, so we continue to focus on 'selective tourism' i.e. looking after family and friends with old fashioned hospitality, ensuring that contracts will be renewed for the following year.

We cannot raise revenue through taxes as all nationalised Horswellians already selflessly donate their entire income to the Exchequer for the good of the country. Looking at ways to attract Foreign Currency, we are thinking of hiding a speed camera in the hydrangeas to catch unwitting motorists flirting the gravel from the drive into the bushes. Our spin-doctors have advised us it would not look good if we were seen to be the first offenders.

As you can imagine, the Chancellor, with his lifetime's involvement in farming, has strong views regarding Horswellia's Agricultural Policy. Recent forays beyond our own borders have shown that 'set-aside' and 'conservation' are all too frequently euphemisms for neglect and despair in the countryside. In Horswellia, intense cultivation is still very much the order of the day, with only woodlands and hedgerows designated as wildlife sanctuaries.

Should there be cross-border scuffles, the Sea Gulls, with their aerial lookout on our rooftop, can be our Bomber Command. Their accuracy, as yet, cannot be guaranteed. The black streaks of misplaced incendiaries splashed on our walls are evidence of their need for further target practice. We also have our own Fleet Air Arm: Mrs. Duck's eleven fluffy babies have grown into ten big, healthy ducks, their youthful squeaks now developed into resounding quacks. Until now they have been confined to barracks to protect them from the predation of a wily fox. But, as soon as they 'have their wings' they will be released back onto the pond to take their chance. Meanwhile, under Mrs. Duck's careful tutelage they spend their days square-bashing in the main courtyard, practising parachute landings off the steps and learning basic survival skills. Hopefully they will be a force to be reckoned with by the time they have to confront 'the enemy'. Like any Commander-in-Chief, we are loathe to send 'Our Boys' over the top into hostile territory. We fear mass fatalities. But, our Grey Indian Runner is about to hatch her eggs so it will be only a matter of days before we have to make room for the new clutch of recruits.

The Peafowl, now known as the Generals, are not too happy at having to share their parade ground with all these flat-footed troops. They have managed to ensure their place at the top of the pecking order, with lots of puffed-up pride and a firm refusal to come to Dinner in anything other than full Dress Uniform with Medals displayed, but behind their backs the troops giggle and cackle mischievously in a corner.

In Horswellia, Wimbledon Fortnight will be a National Holiday, the Chancellor will be allowed a day off for the World Cup Final and every Sunday shall be a day of rest. Apart from that, every day will feel like a holiday because our fate will be determined by ourselves and fellow Horswellians, not by imperial edict from a bombproof bunker in Washington or Whitehall. Instead we'll be free – free to do what we like – and to make our own mistakes!

34

SEPTEMBER 2002

First there was August…

———◆◉◉◉◆———

First there was August; bright, brash, and bustling with visitors, and then September, if not a full stop at least a semi-colon in the syntax of the year. A pause for us to draw breath before the onrush of Autumn. Suddenly there is a stillness, a welcome peace when the golden days of late summer return the countryside to those who live here and we can resume the usual pattern of our lives.

But how empty the house feels without the paraphernalia of grand-children: their surfboards and wetsuits, beach towels and trainers, the buckets and spades and cuddly toys. How empty the beach has become without all the airbeds and inflatable boats, the picnic rugs, hampers, windbreaks and tents. Even the lanes seem empty now that all the 4-wheel drives and people carriers no longer squeeze by, laden to the roof with children and possessions.

After a month of visitors there is a lot to catch up on: housework, laundry, bills to pay, letters to write, gardening to do. With work every-where we look it is hard to know where to begin. Or where to find the energy. Survival tactics are clearly required: We decide to eat up all the leftover children's food, maximising our intake of additives and e-numbers in the hope of becoming hyperactive.

Charming childish thank you letters soon arrive, their colourful drawings and mis-spelt (mis-spelled?) words make us smile. Memories slide through our heads projecting images of sand castles and seaweed fights, icy water and electric squeals. What fun we had! And despite our exhaustion, how sad we were to see them go!

The dogs leap with joy to resume their walks to the beach. Selfishly we love it when all the visitors have gone. When all that is left is a curve of sand and the sigh and hiss of the sea. Bertie is always first into the water. He lowers himself gently into the shallows until deliciously cool, then races up the beach like a mad thing sending up a flurry of sand. Flossie swims out around the rocks, snapping at her own bow wave and has to be cajoled from the water to continue our journey. The hedgerows are tired and tangled now, providing protection for ripening brambles and fat black sloes. Spiders' webs hold morning dew and sunlight gleams on metallic wings as horseflies doze.

Some days it feels so still it is as if the whole world is holding its breath. High pressure days, when the air is so clear one can see the definition of each individual pebble, the shape of every leaf, the detail of far-distant views that go on forever. Days when dragonflies skim the surface of the pond, and bees drone by intent on honey. When dandelion clocks and thistledown drift like feathers on the wind and squirrels scamper across the lawn filling their winter larders with supplies. The sun, still hot upon our skin, encourages us to sit outside and absorb its warmth. We sit, like used batteries left on a radiator, hoping to recharge ourselves sufficiently to last through the winter.

On other days, winds storm through the trees like a tidal wave. With a deafening roar they swirl and toss the leaf-laden branches in an attempt to relieve them of their burden. But they are too early. The leaves rattle their defiance and hold on tight. Disappointed, the winds race on through the garden, scattering rose petals and teasing the peafowl with their bullying strength.

In passing, the winds shake the apples from the trees with a bruising thump, reminding me there is chutney to be made. Peeling apples used to be a chore, but now with my American Apple Peeler (A gift from my Oregon Aunt) it has become a pleasure. A few turns of the handle and not only is the apple neatly peeled and cored but sliced as well. It may not be rocket science but it's a gadget no country kitchen should be without.

It seems such obvious good husbandry to utilise one's own produce when it is available that the lack of support for the British Agricultural Industry defies logic. It is evident that those who make the rules are not countrymen. The policy to import wheat from the Ukraine and milk from Poland, both from unmonitored sources whilst our own yields are good and production methods proven to be of the highest quality, beggars belief. Why are we destroying the things we do well? Why is it so 'unfashionable' to protect our own industries, whilst supporting others? Why are we not allowed to be proud of Great Britain? Does it no longer exist?

'Africa' our Prime Minister stated at the World Earth Summit in Johannesburg 'Is my passion'. Well, that is all fine and dandy, except what we need is someone who has a passion for our own country. Let Africans be passionate about Africa, and please, please, let Britons, and especially our leaders, be passionate about Britain.

In the Times this week there was a scathing article about the nationalistic flag waving which accompanies the Last Night of the Proms. Why is it laudable to sing and wave flags in support of a football team and yet not at a concert? Why is it acceptable to attend a World Cup Final with faces painted as national emblems, to hurl abuse at the competing teams from other countries, to sing Rule Britannia from the stands and yet not to support our country elsewhere? We ARE our country. If we are not prepared to honour it, we are failing to honour ourselves.

35

CHRISTMAS 2002

Kiss and tell…
Giants felled

———◉◉◉———

One way and another it has been a colourful Autumn, with drama, tantrums and storms rampaging through the real world of nature and the artificial creations of the media. In both cases individuals have been undermined by the onslaught, with their strength and credentials being severely tested.

It is not over yet. Look out for further startling revelations to the press: Bertie, encouraged by the tasteless outpourings of Princess Diana's former butler, is preparing to release his diaries, charting his life since leaving the sanctuary of Davidson and Prosser's Veterinary Establishment (The Priory Clinic of the Canine world) where he was being treated for abandonment and abuse by an unnamed aggressor, and his subsequent rise to a position of priviledge and favour within 'The Household'.

Entitled 'What the Briard Saw' it is expected to reveal tantalising gossip of an intimate nature. Having turned down substantial offers from the West Alvington Weekly, the Chillington Chin-Wag and Woof! Magazine he has negotiated an undisclosed sum for his memoirs by exploiting his owner's connection with the Village Voic magazine. Needless to say, fear of betrayal is sending shock waves through 'The Family'.

It is thought that Bertie has never fully recovered from the death of his favorite Labrador and dearest friend Abo. Only now, after years of sharing the same basket, have his true feelings been made known. Unfairly accused of stealing Abo's personal items, including his bowl, rubber ball, lead and blanket in the emotional aftermath of his hero's death, Bertie is expected to use his diaries to clear his name.

'What the Briard Saw' will contain allegations which neither 'The Family', nor the deceased can now disprove, casting an unpleasant light on the behaviour of a dog once widely respected and admired. Disclosures regarding night-time assignations and unsuitable liaisons could easily be verified by the many kind-hearted people who, finding him wandering the streets without money or identification, discreetly returned him to 'The Household'. Observations that the deceased once went out for 'a night on the tiles' wearing only a black fur coat could prove particularly difficult to deny. The testimony of the local dog catcher will confirm that it was still being worn when he visited the miscreant at the Ipplepen Dog Pound and Remand Centre the following morning. 'The Family' are hoping to halt further embarrassing revelations by offering the Editor of the Village Voice substantial enticements to cancel publication. Terms of the deal are expected to include a promise to try even harder to meet editorial deadlines!!

Meanwhile Flossie the Sheepdog has been seen lying in her basket in a provocative page three manner preparing for her 'kiss and tell' expose of lust and licks with the Manager of the Canine Football team. A book and film deal are apparently imminent (Dependant on owner's commission).

While 'The Family' have been nursing the fragile egos of minor celebrity the garden has been facing storms of a different kind. Lightening strikes and gale force winds have left their mark. On the basis that lightening never strikes twice in the same place, my husband has ordered a further 1,000 bulbs and resumed his bluebell planting in the woods. His previous efforts were abruptly curtailed when an enormous ash tree was struck to the ground on the very spot where he had been working only seconds before. The timing of this catastrophic descent and my husband's narrow escape proves that God does indeed work in mysterious ways: The call of nature should never be ignored!

Obviously the preservation of a husband is considerably more important than the loss of a tree, but that is not to underestimate our sadness at losing such a venerable giant. After two days of valiant battle another tree, an ancient sycamore, was also defeated, its huge trunk wrenched in two by the brute force of the wind. It crashed down the bank onto the pond scattering a flurry of terrified ducks into the sky as its branches disappeared beneath the water. 'Plenty of good firewood' a visitor remarked, bringing necessary practicality to our sense of bereavement.

And so, whilst elsewhere the air is full of gossip and dissent, talk of war, and threats to the monarchy, here the air is abuzz with the sound of chainsaws and the clattering, snapping metal jaws of the shredder devouring brushwood and spitting it into woodchips. With aching limbs and heavy hearts we watch the mighty trees reduced to mulch for the garden and logs for the woodshed. Either way, here or in London, history is being destroyed, giants are picked over by the little people and reduced to ash.

It is not only the Monarchy under attack. It is all forms of tradition, from the Inns of Court and the Opening of Parliament to Private Education and Country Pursuits. Pomp and Ceremony are decried in favour of sleek modernity, while technical advances outweigh interpersonal relationships. And who can stop the tide? With an uncertain future of suicide bombers, snipers, dirty bombs and anthrax scares to look forward to, one thing remains unchanged: The halls of Horswell will be decked with holly, fir trees will bristle with tinsel and bows, and the spirit of Christmas, of Peace, Love and Fellowship will do its utmost to prevail.

In the words of Sir Walter Scott: 'Heap on more wood! The wind is chill; But let it whistle as it will, We'll keep our Christmas merry still.'

A safe and merry Christmas to you all !

36

JANUARY 2003

Seize the day!

———◦◉◦———

Several years ago I was invited by a wealthy Indian client to inspect the new 'Queen Anne-style Manor House' that he was building for his family. The house, he told me, was to be completed in time for his son's wedding, three weeks hence. He asked me if I would advise on the placement of his furniture and household possessions. These were due to be flown over, by chartered aeroplane from Singapore, arriving just 24 hours before the wedding!!

When I arrived on site, I was shocked to discover that the house was still at the breeze block stage of construction, with neither staircase, doors or window frames yet in place. It was a large house, on three floors. A mansion. Although now surrounded by the usual chaos of a busy building site it would undoubtedly be an extremely handsome house when eventually completed.

'What do you think?' he asked.

'Amazing!' I replied absorbing the vast scale of the project. Then added: 'But there's no way it can be finished in three weeks. That would be impossible.'

'It will be ready.' He pronounced without a quiver of doubt. 'There is a hefty penalty clause written into the contract. The builder knows it must be ready on time.'

I shook my head in astonishment, pitying the builder.

'You will see it when you come to help with the furniture.' He said. 'It will be ready. I promise you.'

I thought his faith in British workmen was admirable, to say the very least.

'Now,' he continued, 'Tell me. Do you not think it is very beautiful?'

I have always found it hard to tell a lie. He was watching me closely.

'I think it is going to be very beautiful...' I began, trying to choose my words carefully.

'Except?' he asked tartly, picking up on my hesitation.

'Except' I continued 'The sills of the windows are all too high; the proportion is wrong and from the inside it must be hard to enjoy the views of the surrounding countryside. They would look much better if they were lowered by one course of blockwork.'

My client called a man towards him and introduced him to me: 'This is my builder.'

He turned to the builder and to my intense embarrassment said 'My Interior Designer says the windows all need lowering. Please remove one course of blockwork from each and alter the windows accordingly.'

The builder was a large man. He had hands the size of shovels. How he restrained himself from snapping me in two I shall never know. He must have been paralysed with rage. I can still feel the shockwaves of murderous intention that emanated from him like steam from a pressure cooker.

I am reminded of this now because, as I write, kitchen plans and lighting circuits are arriving by e-mail from our younger daughter who is anxious about various aspects of the work currently in progress at her home. It has become something of a Sunday habit. After our weekends of lengthy telephone discussions and reciprocal e-mailing, it is guaranteed that there will be certain 'adjustments' to be made in the week ahead. Her builders must hate Mondays!

Is it really possible that Christmas can have come and gone so fast? It seemed to race upon us like a tidal wave and then subside all too quickly in a tumultuous backwash of used wrapping paper and wilting decorations.

Suddenly, here we are in the New Year, not knowing whether to greet its new opportunities with our usual vigour, or whether to regard the number of troops massing on the borders of Iraq as grains of sand in an hour glass, counting us down to the end of time.

Optimism, under the present circumstances is hard to find. The media bombard us daily with their doubts and fears. Those who have already experienced the horrors of earlier wars, pray for peace while young men and women in the armed forces say fond farewells to their families, unsure of what will be required of them; to engage in battle or to retreat. Somehow I do not see President Bush in the role of the Grand Old Duke of York. Having 'marched his men to the top of the hill' I think it will be almost impossible to 'march them down again' without a fight.

The house looks so bare now that the Christmas trees have been removed, and the days are losing their colour as we resume our routines and try to appease our indignant, overfed digestive systems. A new year's resolution sees me swimming half a mile before breakfast then sitting all day at my computer. I am determined to finish 'the novel' which has proved to be a considerable log-jam in our lives over the past two years. All socialising is banned for the month of January. I am in self imposed 'book purdah', and despite the tempting brochures strewn around my desk, unable to even contemplate an escape to the sun until I have written the last word of the final chapter.

And then, even when the actual writing is finished, it is still only the beginning of another long and painful process of finding a publisher. I have days when I could throw it all, happily, into the waste basket, and other days when I see it splashed across our cinema screens and me, congratulating Nicole Kidman at the Oscars Ceremony for her portrayal of my leading character! Who can tell what may happen? But one thing is for sure, if I don't give it a try, I will never know.

To ease my 'solitary' confinement I have made my office as comfortable as possible, with flowers, a heater, music and plenty of light. With the dark frosty days we have been having it has undoubtedly become the cosiest place in the house to be. Initially my longsuffering husband had imagined having to mount a guard to prevent me from escaping. Instead he is now frequently to be found, with the two dogs, scratching at the door and whimpering to come in! So here we are, the four of us who live in this great big house, jammed in a room no bigger than a dog-kennel; the dogs stretched out in front of the fire, my husband on the sofa having a post gardening, post meridian nap and me at the key board!

My pre-breakfast forays into the outside world have given me a new perspective on life. 6.30 a.m. has never been my finest hour! But now, clothed in a damp swimsuit and a woolly scarf, I set off into the cold dark mornings like Captain Oates, scaring the owls and startling half frozen pigeons from their roosts. In the headlights I see the ducks still sleeping on the island with their heads tucked under one wing, and beside the drive, the spikey silhouettes of emerging snowdrops. As the air lightens to a steely grey, I enjoy the black lace of leafless trees etched against a cold sky, and the watchful eye of a blackbird as she flies ahead of me across the lane. I can see the distinctive shape of magpies as they chatter in the hedgerows looking for carrion. They fly to the ground as soon as I have passed, scavenging for food in my tracks.

At that hour of the day there is a stillness, a purity, a special peace. It is a world untouched by man, where ice holds nature in its iron grip and frost glistens in the morning light. Half awake I may be, but there is still a wealth of beauty to be found. And on my return, weak limbed and red faced from exertion, there is warmth and breakfast and newspapers to enjoy, and a whole perfect day ahead of me.

So, whatever lies ahead, be it peace or war, let us be thankful for today and make the most of every moment. In the words of Horace: 'Carpe diem, quam minimum credula postero' – Seize the day! having only the smallest trust in tomorrow.

37

MARCH 2003

Flower-power revisited

———◦◦◦◦———

Clothes festoon the walls and cupboards of our dressing room, the hastily discarded costume changes of the past few weeks, waiting to be put away. Wedding outfits, hats and shoes mingle with evening dresses, party frocks, morning suits and white tie and tails reminding us of special friends and elegant events. It has been a hectic time, blurred by frantic journeys flying up and down the M5. If it were possible to collect air miles by travelling on a motorway, we would have earned a free trip to the moon by now.

Meanwhile, on the home front, endless visitors have left us with heaps of laundry that resemble the snow capped ranges of the Himalayas, and larders and cellars that look distinctly bare. Not that I am down-hearted by all the ironing that lies ahead. On the contrary, I am expecting a rush of energy at any moment. Nor am I unduly worried about our depleted booze supplies (My husband has a tame bat that guards those anyway!) Why am I so insouciant, so uncomplaining? Well, having been screened for food sensitivities and vitamin and mineral deficiencies I am now on a new regime. According to my diagnosis I am, for three whole months, to avoid: wheat, yeast, tea, coffee, dairy products, sugar, beef, peanuts and, as if that were not bad enough, alcohol as well !! In exchange for this appalling deprivation I am assured that I will have organs that work perfectly, a squeaky clean liver and a much needed surge in my energy levels.

The consultant is a nice, intelligent woman. I want to believe her. Besides, her fees would have bought us a decent meal at the Savoy and I don't want to go hungry for nothing. I think I could have managed a wheat-free diet, or a sugar-free diet, perhaps even an alcohol-free diet, but everything (Or rather, nothing) all at the same time?? What is there left for heavens sake?? I now stand peering into the recesses of fridge and larder desperate to find something I can eat. I ask you: 'Is it possible to survive for three months on rice cakes and elderflower tea?'

In the garden the air is alive with the song of birds staking out their territory. Already they are in pairs and busy ferrying twigs to build their nests. Blackbirds, a robin, blue tits, a wren and a pheasant join our peacocks for breakfast outside the French Windows. On the other side of the glass the dogs, Bertie and Flossie, watch with interest without scaring them away. Meanwhile, I swallow another handful of vitamins and munch on an oatcake, trying not to envy them their peanuts and breadcrumbs.

The ducks are making nests all around the garden, some hidden under bushes, others behind trees or tucked into grassy hollows. With Monsieur Renard taking nightly strolls up the driveway they will need all the cover and camouflage they can find. Goldfish, a generous present from Sally and her daughter Alice, now swim in the large pond. On sunny days we can see a glimpse of silver or gold amongst the green weed as Flash and Jaws swim with their friends, exploring their new home.

The snowdrops are nearly over now but there are violets, primroses and daffodils to take their place. They look wonderful beneath the camellias, spreading up into the woods. I read somewhere that daffodils are edible, primroses too. So, if I get really hungry, I can always forgo the tofu and soya milk and rely on flower power instead!

Thinking of flower power reminds me of the hippy days of the early seventies. My sister and I drifted footloose and fancy free across America, driving the slow route from New York on the east coast to San Francisco on the West. Hawaii was the next stop. I remember clearly our arrival in Honolulu airport. The baggage hall was crowded with groups of young boys in uniform. They appeared tense and uncertain, with pale faces and eyes round with fear. Summer school, I thought, or maybe the first day of term. Their anxiety haunted me.

It was several days later that I discovered they were not school boys, but the latest intake of conscripts drafted in to fight the Vietnam war. To me, at twenty years old, they looked like children.

My sister and I shared a large rambling house on St. Louis Heights overlooking Honolulu with eight other young people: Five girls and five boys between the ages of 20 and 23. All of we girls worked to pay the rent, while the boys were all Vietnam veterans on final Rest and Recuperation waiting to be sent 'home'. During the day the boys stayed at the house or went to the beach to smoke dope and reminisce. In the evenings we would take it in turns to cook, and then eat Dinner together as a 'family'. The conversation would start with 'surfing' but always end with 'war'. Again and again they would go over the details of every battle, every manoeuvre, trying to rationalise their actions and expunge the cruellest memories from their minds.

All remembered in graphic detail their first 'kill', especially the civilians: The mother with her baby strapped to her back planting rice in a paddy field, caught in the crossfire between North and South Vietnamese; the child sent into their camp to beg for food, volatile explosives hidden under his clothes. None could forget the horrors they had witnessed and none felt able to move on. They had been plucked from their loving families and gentle, civilised lifestyles to be dropped, after negligible training, into the hell of war. Afterwards, they felt unable to return to their 'apple-pie' mothers and neat suburban homes; they were changed men, their lives damaged or destroyed by their call to arms. Of our five house-mates, only two ever made it home.

As yet, the men we are sending to Iraq are not conscripts but trained men who have chosen the armed forces for a career, but when I see their young brave faces on the television the memories come flooding back. Above all I pray for their homecoming, that the welcome they receive makes the battles they have fought worthwhile. I have seen how important it is that the difficulties of re-integration with their families and friends are understood and made easier to bear. Like Vietnam, a war with Iraq is an 'unpopular' war; it lacks the full support of the nation. But whether or not war is ever justified, the men who make up that fighting force deserve every ounce of our admiration and respect. As civilians we have the luxury of our opinions and the freedom of our actions. The armed forces have orders to follow and lives that will be changed forever.

38

MAY 2003

London has changed…

—◦◦◦—

London has changed. It is now so cosmopolitan that its quintessential Englishness seems under threat. In shops expensive purchases are now overshadowed by the watchful glare of omnipresent store detectives, and on the streets, despite the plethora of exotic clothes for sale, the dress is uniformly drab, with even the smallest flash of gold jewellery eliciting mean and hungry looks. Waiters, shop assistants and bus conductors seem all to be immigrants of eastern European origins. Even the purveyors of tourist souvenirs sell their gaudy wares with barely a word of English evident during the transaction, and the Union Jacks decorating their stalls unashamedly proclaim that they are 'Made in China'. The congestion charge has so reduced the number of private vehicles on the streets that the atmosphere is strangely impersonal with none of the noisy 'buzz' of the old confusion. There may be less traffic, but the traffic that remains seems slower than ever, enabling taxi drivers with a philosophical bent to warm at length to their theme.

My cabbie was not a happy man: 'It's disgustin' he shouts over his shoulder as he tries to simultaneously out-manoeuvre a Mercedes full of Arabs and a double-decker bus. 'Wot these politicians are doin' to this country. Givin' it away, that's wot they're doin', giving away everything our fathers fought for, everything that makes all these blooming foreigners want to come here in the first place! It's the end of our democracy and we can't do a thing about it. They don't listen. We're impotent. That's wot I feel. Impotent!'

The bus and the Mercedes converge squeezing us to a shuddering halt.

'Best blooming country in the world and they want to give it all away. Tell us we've got to become part of the United States of Europe. Wot for? Wot have they ever done for us?'

The lights change and the tirade continues. 'You know what? They're giving these asylum seekers a car allowance now.'

'They are?' I venture, clinging on to my seat as we swirl around Hyde Park Corner and rattle down the Mall.

'Yeah and some of them have clubbed together and bought themselves a bloomin' Range Rover haven't they. No one ever gave me a bloomin' Range Rover did they? And I've worked here all me bloomin'life!'

We slice through the newly pedestrianised Trafalgar Square, past the queues for the Titian exhibition at the National and the barriers of continuing road works and slip gratefully into the calm of Whitehall and the sanctuary of the Farmer's Club.

'What's the answer?' I ask as I pay my fare.

'Dunno' he replies 'It's too late, innit? It's not our country any more, innit? Nah! It belongs to them, the politicians. They don't care about us anymore. They do just what they like. Me and the Missus we can't take any more. As soon as our Julie's finished her Master's degree we're off, leaving.'

'Where will you go?' I ask.

'Spain, we've already got a house there. It's not about the Euro is it, it's about the quality of life.'

And he's right: it is not about the Euro, it's about all that accompanies it – the irrevocable changes to our way of life that are being made without our consent, changes so extreme that they undermine the democracy of this country and hand power to an unelected body of

European Commissioners; power that affects our freedom and security, our homes and our pensions, power which once given no future English government can ever regain.

Historically London was always a haven for villains and thieves. For centuries pick-pockets and conmen have been adept at creating a diversion to distract attention from their sleight of hand. But this time it is more serious. It is our politicians who are using smoke and mirrors, relying on the current brouhaha about the Euro to distract our attention from the greatest deceit of all time.

Thankfully at home, in rural Horswellia, life continues in its usual pattern for this time of year: Too much rain and too little sun. Too many weeds and too few flowers. Too much to do and too little time. And, as always, visitors are imminent. Whereas some gardens are famous for their hostas or their collection of clematis, ours at the moment must house the finest collection of nettles and docks in the South West. Primarily a Spring garden, now that the rhododendron, azaleas, camellias, magnolia and cherry blossoms are over everything looks decidedly green. Infuriatingly we must wait for the daffodils, primroses and bluebells to die back before we can cut the long grass where they have flowered. The weeds take unfair advantage of our hesitation and tempt us to attack them with the strimmer before it is time, but we have learned that it is best to wait.

The rabbits still plague the herbaceous borders, devouring any plant we fail to surround with wire, but with a little warmth to swell the buds the peonies, iris and roses should soon be flowering, and the lime green froth of alchemilla mollis begin to overflow the blue catmint, pink geranium and London Pride. Behind them an ancient wisteria festoons the wall with long racemes of purplish blue. Beneath, a snake coils slowly through the trellis and slithers towards its hole under the roots, barely distinguishable in thickness and in colour from the grey and woody stems.

Around the pond variegated hostas, blue iris and white dicentra look pretty against the dark purple leaves of blue prunella and citrus euphorbia. By the waterfall the new fronds of the Tasmanian Fern Trees are beginning to uncurl and the gunnera are already holding out their giant leaves to catch the rain. Beyond, brilliant candelabra primulas and white zantedeschia compete with a pretty variegated pond weed that threatens to invade the entire area, and on the island six drakes snooze uneasily dreaming of foxes or of finding a mate.

A few weeks ago we were rewarded with the idyllic sight of a small deer tiptoeing around the back of the pond. We watched it slowly make its way along the path, grazing amongst the primroses, quite untroubled by our presence. It was a magical scene and we felt priviledged to have been visited by something so lovely.

When there is so much beauty to be found in the world around us one wonders why so many modern artists seem inspired only by all that is squalid and degenerate. The Saatchi collection now housed in Red Ken's palace, City Hall, beside the great wheel of the London Eye, typifies all that is ugly. Even the shock value which attracted so much attention when they first appeared at the Summer Exhibition of the Royal Academy has faded into a sad statement of a soulless culture. The formaldehyde of Damien Hirst's pickled animals is growing cloudy, their grey flesh beginning to decompose and the menace of the Myra Hindley portrait painted with children's handprints is tempered by the knowledge that she can no longer do us harm. In the gloomy surroundings of City Hall Tracy Emmin's 'Unmade Bed' is even more sordid than I had remembered and Muerke's stark sculptures of the human form, although brilliant in technique, seemed tragically vulnerable and remote.

No wonder Mr. Saatchi wanted to rid his home of this depressing collection. Compared to the vibrant artistry of the paintings by Titian that still delight today's art lovers four hundred years after they were painted, this collection is surely redundant.

39

July 2003

I'm late, I'm late…

———⊷◉◉◉⊶———

I'm late, I'm late, for a very important date! Tomorrow we're going to print and here I sit at the eleventh hour wondering where the months have flown and why, when the days have been so full, the pages of the Horswell Diary are still so empty! As I flick back through my memory I see a blur of friends and family, images of frantic gardening and hectic housework. I recall the aches and pains of long car journeys, feel the warmth of summer sunshine and hear the gaiety of laughter and spirited conversation.

So where did all our days disappear? It all began six months ago, when, in a moment of weakness, we agreed to host a visit from the members of the Devon Gardens Trust. Surely, we thought at the time, by the second of June we will have everything looking attractive, so why not? But we had underestimated the work to be done, and, misjudging the inexorable intrusion of our social life, we had overestimated the time we would have available to work in the garden.

Inevitably, the week immediately before our visitors' arrival we were weeding around the clock and wondering why we had ever agreed to the idea. Late flowering daffodils, bluebells and cowslips meant we were unable to cut all of the long grass and a spell of wet weather hindered our progress – as did a night in Oxfordshire to attend an 80th Birthday party, a day out with K.E.D.F.A.S. to visit Wells Cathedral and a stylish evening drinking champagne to celebrate something we can't quite remember at the Royal Western Yacht Club on Queen Anne's Battery in Plymouth.

However, although far from the perfection we might have wished to present, the gardens seemed to meet with the approval of our distinguished guests, and for those for whom our efforts may have fallen short of expectations there were copious quantities of tea and cake which hopefully softened their judgement. Everyone was very kind and we all had a wonderfully happy, if exhausting, day. In fact I think I may have discovered a new formula for world peace: Gardening.

Over the years I have noticed how gardening is a language which transcends all barriers, all differences and all ages. A true love of flowers, of structure and form, an eye for colour, an awareness of light and shade and the changing seasons gives common ground to conversations with total strangers, promoting instant friendship and stimulating lively debate. Not only does gardening give us hope and humility, patience and respect but it reminds us of our own transience and our human limitations. What other 'language' can offer so much?

The day after The Visit, we hung up our gardening gloves, packed our suitcases and left for France. French, as we all know, has to be pronounced perfectly before a Frenchman will condescend to understand someone from England. It was a good thing therefore that the sixteen people who joined us for lunch at our hotel in Chenonceau were those responsible for teaching me their language in the first place. Any mistakes would have to be forgiven.

As a child I had stayed for a month each year with this family, welcomed as an 'adopted' daughter by Eliane whose four boys teased me like brothers. Now those boys are grown men with adult children of their own. They have become serious and successful, their teenage antics happy memories for us all to reconstruct, exaggerate and embellish. Aunts and cousins added colour to our recollections and children shook their heads with disbelief. Laughter flowed around the table, a language of its own.

The lunch was originally convened at the time of the war in Iraq, when tensions between Mr. Blair and Mr. Chirac were at their worst. 'Pour consolider l'amitie Franco-Britannique' we wrote on the invitations that we sent. Inevitably, in a country where politics quicken the blood, discussion soon turned to the reasons for war. 'Why?' They asked. 'We thought Mr. Blair was a good man. Now we think he is just like Mr. Bush.'

I veered away from a contentious topic and asked how they liked the Euro. We all agreed that life in France has become very much more expensive since the currency has changed. Some said the opportunities for increased trade are good for France, others that the economy is poor and if there were another referendum today the vote would be 'Non!' All agreed vehemently that they could see no advantage for Britain if it were to join. 'You have a different mentality' they said 'You are like the Americans' 'We are continentals, used to crossing each others borders, they are our neighbours, our friends.'

'But what if your armed forces were lead into battle by commanders of a different nationality?' I asked, 'Are the French not too proud for that?'

'Soldiers are soldiers.' They reply. 'They are paid to follow orders. They will not mind'.

'Even if those orders emanate from an unelected, undemocratic European Commission?' I asked, pressing for a stiffer reaction. They reply with a Gallic shrug of their shoulders:

'There have always been politicians, there have always been laws. We may not always agree with them but we are still here.'

It seemed a very un-English reaction and I desisted from further questions for fear of upsetting the entente cordiale.

As a country I fear we have lost a lot of respect over our involvement in Iraq. The stoical English Bulldog has been replaced by an hysterical Chihuahua snapping at the heels of history, anxious for recognition.

Moving on to the subject of dogs, while in the interests of hygiene I am happy to pooper scoop deposits our dogs make on the beach, I am not prepared to pick up the metal trays of discarded barbecues or the bags of babies' nappies that now litter the sand dunes. Hopefully the National Trust and the Council have come to a practicable solution to the lack of waste disposal facilities and our children and grandchildren can once again enjoy building sandcastles or burying Auntie Mabel without the fear of digging up someone else's remains!

In France, a 'Taxe de Sejour' is imposed on all tourists, payable via their hotel/accommodation bills. The money collected goes directly to the Mayor of that region who is then responsible for spending it on improvements that will make the area more attractive to visitors and thus further boost the local economy. It is rare in France to see litter. Towns and villages often overflow with flowers; trees are regularly planted to soften harsh landscapes and pavements are transformed into attractive terraces for sidewalk cafes. Investment in their environment is clearly evident and with it a 'joie de vivre', a sense of well being that is often missing in this country. I was incensed to read in an English newspaper that the flag of St. George was ordered to be removed from outside a Town hall recently 'for fear of causing offence to other nationals'. Have you ever heard anything so ridiculous? A little pride in our poor country would do wonders for our battered morale.

Since our return, like so many of us who live in this beautiful part of the world, we have been inundated with visits from family and friends. Exhausted we may be, but all are precious and we are sad when it is time for them to leave. 'Friends', I read somewhere, 'are they who keep alive your faith in human nature, that make you believe that it is a good universe. They are the antidote to despair, the elixir of hope, the tonic for depression. Give to them without reluctance.' And so we must, aware of our good fortune.

40

September 2003

Quinces, yellow and knobbly…

—◦◦◦—

The sight of quinces yellow and knobbly upon the tree has sent me back to the house for a basket. Already, in my mind's eye I can see them converted into semi-precious jewels: gleaming jars of rose-quartz nectar, fragrant and sweet as pollen to a bee. I scour the house in search of my jelly-making bag and find it, like a moth in a chrysalis, jammed in the corner of a drawer. Over the years it has lost its pristine whiteness, dyed with fruits of all description. A clean replacement would probably be inexpensive but I prefer it as it is. There's history in this bag, the tradition of a jam-maker's art handed down from generation to generation, from my grandmother to me. I can see her now: cheeks pink from the heat of the stove, blue eyes twinkling beneath a haze of white hair as she stirs her sugared fruit around the pan.

It was a ritual, an annual rite of magic, an alchemy that witnessed as a child impressed itself upon my mind. I cannot carry the willow basket filled with fruit or hear the heavy clank of the preserving pan's handle without seeing my grandmother's hand upon it. Nor shall I see the rows of finished preserves without remembering her weary sigh of satisfaction and gentle look of quiet pride.

For me jam-making is a time for 'roots' and remembrance; a cosy, heart-warming occupation that celebrates the bounty of another year. Last week my mother helped me pick stones from 5kg of damsons. Our hands red-stained from their cooked juice, our backs aching as we stood at the kitchen worktop, we talked and reminisced and put the world to rights, enjoying each other's company.

It is more than simply making jam, it is about storing memories in a bottle. It is potting history in a jar. Many months from now just a single mouthful of that damson jam will enable us to dip into the past as easily as a spoon into jelly, its taste dissolving on our tongues a sweet reminder of our happy day.

What a wonderful summer we have had! Hot sunshine and blue skies have distracted us from tawdry politics and boosted morale enabling us to relax and enjoy the things we hold dear: family and friends, our garden, the beach, the beauty of the countryside, being able to eat outside, warm starry nights, salads and shellfish and chilled rose wine.

Despite the lack of rain the garden has remained amazingly lush and green. Only now are hints of drought and autumn creeping in: Spiders' webs fine-spun across the lawn, sparkling with morning dew; sycamore leaves dry and crisp, the first to fall, clattering through the branches; squirrels brazenly stealing nuts and leaving teethmarks in the pears that ripen on the tree. Colour is disappearing from the flower beds and hydrangea heads are turning brown. Beneath the trees woodland cyclamen are small this year and in the orchard fruits, though plentiful, lack their usual rain-swelled girth.

As ever there is work to be done, borders to tidy, plants to cut back, climbers to restrain, but the fine weather makes gardening a pleasure and the robin's autumn song gives us delightful recompense for the occasional grub or worm revealed by our efforts. The peafowl, having strewn their long tail-feathers untidily hither and thither, look neat and newly shorn. Contentedly they lie beside us in the sun, or trample through the lavender bushes snapping up the small white moths that dance, all too briefly, above their scented blooms.

England has been fortunate compared with those countries where the heat has been even more intense. Although parched in many areas, the countryside has been spared the ravages of forest fire that has deci-mated vast areas of the South of France and the strength of Hurricane

135

Isabel currently raking the eastern seabord of the United States. Whilst we have had to worry only about watering our plants others have suffered earth so dry it has created dust storms and sudden mini tornados. Our friends in the Loire Valley lost not only the roof off their barn but 300 of their 400 walnut trees when a freak storm swirled through their property and tore up the trees by their roots.

For them it is a disaster beyond repair. They are elderly and walnut trees are slow to establish. There is not time for them to see another harvest. The trees were not only their way of life, they were their pension fund. And now they are surrounded by acres of fallen tree trunks with tonnes of worthless unripe nuts scattered across the ground, the cost and effort of reparation too great for them to consider.

By September most of our visitors have returned to their homes and grand-children, endearingly self-conscious in their smart new uniforms, have come to terms with their first days back at school. But, as they say, 'Nature abhors a vacuum' and already Horswell is host to visitors of a different kind. Despite our best efforts to remove them, their persistence is remarkable: Every day we scoop crane flies and spiders from the walls and put them outside. Butterflies flap past our noses on invisible currents of air. They pause to alight on cushions or the backs of chairs then batter their wings against the window panes until we set them free. Bats play hide and seek, peering at us upside-down as they hang from the lamp-shades then swoop down the corridors with alarming speed. A robin flies around the kitchen to attract our attention then perches on the bread-bin awaiting crumbs, and as I write a blackbird has just hopped into the room looking around him with a proprietorial air.

At the moment we all seem to co-habit with relative ease but the moment is undoubtedly looming when the mice make their annual assault on the larder. It is then that we have to draw the line.

I have been feeling a little strange lately – for days I have been hearing the tune 'We wish you a Merry Christmas' as I take the dogs for their morning walk along the beach. I find myself humming along to it and then singing out loud 'And a Happy New Year!' Luckily seagulls are incapable of looking surprised and the dogs have lived with me long enough to accept most of my behaviour as the norm. For a while I thought it might be a form of tinnitus, or perhaps advancing senility? Already we have cars with the registrations B1G TOE and EAR 1 calling at the house to administer treatments various. Dementia and men in white coats can surely not be far behind?

It is not something that you like to mention is it? That you can hear music emanating from your left boot? So the eventual discovery of a small battery-operated device in my Father Christmas socks, (a previously unworn present from the grand-children,) came as a great relief.

I am still swimming four mornings a week. That is to say that my stoical husband prises me out of bed at 6. 30 a.m. and hands me the car keys. The car then negotiates the drive to Kingsbridge and half an hour after our arrival the pain is all over and I am awake and it is time to come home for breakfast. At a minimum of half a mile a day it means that I have now swum a hundred (100!!!!) miles, which for someone as dozy as me in the mornings is rather impressive. It also means that should I ever 'accidently' fall off the back of the cross-channel ferry I should stand a reasonably good chance of getting home before my husband can crack open the insurance policy!

41

CHRISTMAS 2003

Christmas? Already?

———◦◉◦———

Can Christmas really be just around the corner when the countryside is still ablaze with autumn colour? While children everywhere have been busy compiling their Yuletide wish-lists and parents prepare to dig deep into their pockets for the latest computer game we have been distracted by the warmth and sunshine of November days, blissfully unaware of the encroaching festivities. The unseasonal weather has encouraged us to work out of doors where we trim and prune, plant bulbs and rake leaves, inspired by the spectacular autumn colours. Surely this year they have been more beautiful, more intense than ever before? Our garden over the past few weeks has been transformed into a scene from fairyland, a silent firework display of deciduous gold and bronze freeze-framed against a dark background of holly and fir.

Leaves overlooked in their uniform summer green have reclaimed their independence delighting us with their infinite variety. As I write, their colours radiate a joyous beauty luminous with autumn sunshine. The vine-leaves that festoon the kitchen courtyard are falling fast, leaving a trail of hand prints across the cobbles: lemon yellow and citrus green, burgundy, claret, ruby and grape. Sweet-chestnut leaves twist and shimmer like goldfish dangling from a line, then, with a clatter, fall to the ground. A breeze sends them rolling and rattling across the gravel, skipping and scurrying, tumbling head over heels into dips and hollows to die like dampened embers.

Tall firs are garlanded with vibrant creepers, dark pines bedecked with necklaces of gold and gleaming jewels. Grey stone walls freckled and blotched with ochre lichen bask in the unexpected warmth. The sunshine highlights their blemishes and glistens on their old quartz veins. Slate roofs are strewn with the yellowed fishbones of wisteria leaves and woodland paths are paved with gold. Red-berried creepers trail through the winter green of bay and laurel while orange flames engulf the branches of maple and cherry. Leaves cascade from tulip trees and beech, as if a mighty hand has emptied a packet of Corn Flakes over their branches. They collect in golden pools that spread daily across the dew-moist lawn awaiting our attention.

Christmas decorations will have a hard act to follow after beauty such as this.

The peacocks gather on sun-warmed steps to preen their newly emerging tails. They bend iridescent teal blue necks to peck and nibble at offending mites lodged between their feathers. Their new companions, a small flock of guinea fowl, are slowly exploring their new surroundings. At first their bald heads and grey plumage remind one of small turkeys but closer inspection reveals a tufted tiara beginning to grow on their heads and pretty white spots on their feathers. However, if they continue to decimate our plants at the current rate they may soon outstay their welcome and run the risk of being converted into Christmas Lunch or perhaps an elegant hat for Ascot.

The squirrels are fat and furry as they hang upside down stealing nuts from the bird feeder. Only the woodpecker is brave enough to challenge them, taking his turn to sway back and forth before giving way to blue tits and greenfinch. Above me a squall of rooks startles into the air like a burst of gunshot peppered against a blue sky. Their dry 'caw-caw' breaks the silence as their dark silhouettes wheel and soar overhead. Bertie, the Briard, comes and rests his huge head on my lap and Flossie the sheepdog tugs at my arm with her paw. Time to go indoors and prepare some lunch for my hard working husband. (Currently bent double beneath the clerodendrons planting his second sack of daffodils and muttering incantations against the originator of the planting scheme!)

The lunchtime News is full of missing children, murder and mayhem, bringing me back to the real world with a bump. I find it extraordinary that at the same time that I am enraptured by the beauty of sun shining through an autumn leaf there is someone else using those exact same minutes to contemplate perpetrating an atrocity so vile it beggars belief. I suppose we are all capable of being damaged to a greater or lesser extent by our life's experiences, but I do believe that for anyone except the clinically insane, decency is a choice and even a murderer knows right from wrong – even if he chooses to ignore it.

I suppose it could be argued that freedom of thought (including ghastly thoughts) is the basis for a true democracy. Thinking of which I wonder if Michael Howard, the new leader of the Conservative Party will bring democracy back to our politics? Love him or loathe him he appears to be a worthy opponent for Mr. Blair and the country on both sides of the political divide should be grateful that debate and thus democracy looks set to replace the headstrong unilateralism of recent years. I am intrigued to hear that Rupert Murdoch the formidable Press Baron is not necessarily prepared to offer the present government his continued support. He is a shrewd businessman. Does he smell the whiff of change in the air?

Tomorrow I am taking a friend to collect her new Labrador puppy. She is under strict orders from my husband to ensure that I do not return with one for myself. Hopefully they will all already be taken, but if there were a little black dog waiting for a new home... who knows?... how could I refuse? I remember when I went to collect our last Labrador Abo from the kennels and came home with his litter brother Alfie too. The air was blue. The dogs were ignored. Then one day when I was unable to look after them I peeped out of the window and watched my husband lifting first one, then the other into the back of his Range Rover. As he picked them up they wriggled and licked his face, snuggling close against him. When he turned to wave goodbye he was smiling and I knew that from that day onwards they would be accepted as part of the family. I wonder if I dare risk it again? If you see my suitcase and a dog basket at the end of the drive you'll know why!

So Christmas is nearly here, and from the emerging snowdrops and early flowering camellias Spring will not be far behind. How quickly this year has disappeared! Already friends are planning next year's travels to destinations that become ever more exotic: Guatemala, Belize and Honduras to name a few. It is hard to imagine that by the time February arrives I too will be desperate for heat and sunshine and will be reaching for the holiday brochures. For now I am content to hibernate at Horswell, warmed by our log fires and the beauty of our surroundings and looking forward to seeing family and friends at Christmas. From all of us, including the dogs, ducks, peacocks, guinea fowl (and puppy????) our wishes to all of you for a very Merry Christmas and a New Year full of hope and happiness.

Message from Mars

—⟢◉◉◉⟣—

Dear Earthlings

After the excitement of the past few weeks and the slow but perfectly executed touch down to post-Christmas normality, it was tempting to remain immobile on my landing module and enjoy a well-earned rest. But Mission Control would have none of it. 'Now is the time…' came the signal between mouthfuls of champagne and much back-slapping and self-congratulation '…to let the wagons roll! Let the exploration begin!' And so, slowly, I have been unfolding from my turbid post-turkey inertia and taking stock of my preparedness to launch into the unknown and potentially hostile terrain of the year 2004. Looking down at my pallid, partially deflated airbag I fear there is much work to be done. However, after twelve days of self-assessment, spatial gymnastics and gradual re-alignment, here I am rolling down the exit ramp of the year 2003 to sample the alien landscape of the world around me:

Firstly it is not as cold as I had expected, in fact, surprisingly mild for the time of year. Camellias and snowdrops are already in bloom and the buds on daffodils and rhododendrons look fat and full of promise. Guinea fowl mingle happily with the ducks, and peacocks preen their gleaming feathers on sun-warmed steps. So far, so good! Oh but bear with me a moment whilst I re-adjust my main antenna and turn it towards Earth.

'Ah yes, that must be it. I can still hear them cheering at Mission Control. Call me sentimental if you will, but after the recent negativity of war and politics (and not forgetting the sad demise of my dear friend Beagle), the sound of success reverberating through my microphones makes me blush with pride.

Stretching upwards through the rare Horswellian atmosphere with my 'thermal emissions spectrometer' I search unsuccessfully for other hotspots of joy in the universe. The best I can find for the moment is the admission by Jacques Delors, the architect of a united Europe and a single currency, that Britain was indeed correct to take the decision to stay out of the Euro. Ha! It doesn't require a digital brain to see the logic in that! Otherwise things seem little changed: Osama Bin Laden is still issuing threats, Prime Minister Blair is still issuing promises and his government is still issuing automatic penalties for any misdemeanour that can be milked for revenue:

The sight of a man in Kingsbridge bent beside his vehicle holding a ruler nearly stops me in my tracks. Adjusting the focus on my micro-scanner I can clearly see him measuring the distance between the kerb and the wheels of his car to check whether or not he has infringed the 50cm gap allowed! I immediately deploy my speed sensors to ensure that my forward velocity remains at a steady 4cm per second. If the long tentacles of government intervention have already reached South Devon it can't be long before a fixed penalty fine is delivered with the next orbit of the 'Mars Express'.

Picking my way carefully between the rocks, lest they conceal hidden speed cameras, I turn my detectors towards the increasingly prevalent thought police: I find myself in a crazy world where prison warders are afraid to use the term 'black' coffee for fear of being labelled racist and Prime Time television presenters are ousted for words made inflammatory by their lack of context. And yet it is the same world where the British Home Secretary David Blunkett, with a misjudged sense of gravity, confided that his first thought on hearing the news that mass murderer Harold Shipman had 'topped himself' was to 'open a bottle' by way of celebration! It makes my logical robotic brain whirr at the iniquity.

Hold on! Mission Control is sending me a signal. Apparently they have selected specific rocks for me to test for signs of liquid water. I'll head towards the one they have nick-named 'Sashimi'. As I approach with my 'rock abrasion tool' extended my cameras tell me that their name is almost prophetic. It is not a rock, but a dead fish. A salmon, clearly stamped with the words 'Polluted in Scotland'. Half of it has been consumed suggesting that life pre-salmon may indeed have been a possibility. I trundle on through the barren landscape towards another interesting rock formation shaped like a pyramid. I scan it carefully with my 'microscopic imager' sending video footage back to Mission Control for interpretation. My voice detector picks up a long embarrassed silence and then, at last, the confirmation that the 'rocks' are actually a pile of unused military body armour mislaid, according to our Defence Minister, Mr. Hoon, 'due to problems with the army's asset-tracking system.' Oh dear. Even a pre-programmed robot can get depressed at times....

But there are some things even I can't take too seriously:

One is Britney Spears' assurance, after 55 hours of a marriage that was later annulled, that she 'Still believes in the sanctity of marriage.' The other is Geordie Greig, editor of Tatler Magazine, who says: 'Plastic surgery has become an essential part of society. It is quite common at this time of year for a woman to come into a surgery with a cheque for £5,000 from her husband for cosmetic surgery for her Christmas present.' Now what kind of woman, in what kind of world would take a gift like that as a compliment??

Humans make life so complicated. Remind me to thank Mission Control that they made me a mere machine, or as Chris Lewicki, my flight director once said 'a bucket of bolts and parts.' You have to be tough in my line of work. Just give 'em the facts. What good is emotion anyway? Who cares if you care? Look what happened to poor Beagle. He just couldn't hack it. Too sensitive.

That's all for now. 2004 certainly looks like being an eventful year.... I think I had better turn right at the next crater and re-charge my batteries... Oh! What's this? I can see tracks ahead of me... Beagle? Beagle is that you?

Yours ever,

Spirit (of Horswell)

43

MARCH 2004

Slaves and Swahili

Looking out at the crisp frost on the lawn and pulling on yet another layer of clothes it is hard to remember that only a week ago we were relaxing in 92 degrees of sunshine on the white sand beaches of East Africa. Phewee! What a contrast! The hairs on my skin are huddling together for comfort and my hard earned tan is falling from the cold wastelands of my body like flakes of snow. I always knew I was a hothouse flower, an orchid not a daisy, in need of light and warmth, quality nutrients and sensitive care. Not for me the life of a stalwart daffodil boldly smiling in the teeth of a gale, nor the snowdrop's valiant struggle to pierce through winter's unforgiving earth. No, at the very least I suppose I could be a camellia, dreaming of faraway places and sunnier climes as its blooms, brown and bruised by the cold, collect around its feet; fading memories of former glory.

I know I must not complain, but layers of Damart plus sweaters and scarves do little for the libido and even less for my appearance. A new laptop computer means I can give our cold office a miss and crouch in my chair beside the fire as I write. Bertie and Flossie lie beside me, pleased to have us home after our travels. What do they care of windsurfing and safaris, exotic scenery or warm turquoise seas? A walk to the beach and a tin of Pedigree Chum can provide a dog with food for thought indefinitely, and with Guinea Fowl and peacocks roaming the garden who needs to go to the Masai Mara for a game drive?

But the thing is – Africa gets under your skin as easily as its dirt gets under your fingernails. Its colour, its warmth, its people; the richness of its history, the fragility of its future. You can feel its heartbeat flooding through your veins, sense its neediness, and its pride, and hear its gentle cry for help echoing through your mind long after you have left. The recent change of leadership in Kenya has brought with it an air of cautious optimism; the possibility at last of having a government that actually cares about its people, not just the financial rewards of a position in office. Past corruption is freely aired in the local press in an effort to clamp down on future losses. But money and resources are in pitifully short supply and one wonders how long the people can live on promises alone. At least now Primary education is free for all and although the lack of money to pay teachers means that classes can be as large as 50 or 60 pupils, the pride of the children in their spotless hand-me-down uniforms is a delight to see. They know, as they walk to school with their books balanced on their heads, that they are taking the first steps towards a better life. But what is important is that Africans, having completed their education are not tempted to hone their skills elsewhere. Their homeland needs them – desperately.

For centuries, the sunny nature and capacity for hard work of the majority of Kenyans has made them an easy target for exploitation. Even as far back as the 14th century they were being taken as slaves by Arab traders who sailed down the coast in their dhows to trade with the local tribes. Several of those coastal tribes were completely wiped out by the years of slave trading that followed. 'Only the intelligent ones remain' said our friend Clement, with his gleaming smile. 'If they were difficult or clever they were left alone. The traders wanted only biddable slaves, not troublesome ones!'

Although they had their own dialect, each of the coastal tribes were able to understand each other, but it was the gradual integration of the Arabs with the Africans which brought about the use of Swahili (A mixture of their two cultures) as a common language.

We flew one day up to Lamu, an island that hugs the Kenyan coast just south of its border with Somalia. It was here that the Arabs made their first landfall and established a town on the waterfront. As we approached by dhow from a neighbouring island it was easy to imagine that since then little had changed. The town stretched along the low horizon, the domes and arches of Moorish design smothered in flowering vines and Bougainvillea; vibrant splashes of orange, pink and purple against pale crumbling stone. As we drew closer we could see the waterfront was a hive of activity, the thrub, thrub, thrub of our diesel engine the only discordant note in a timeless scene

Climbing up stone steps worn thin with age we arrived, incongruous in our western clothes, into a scene seemingly unaltered since the 14th century:

Men in Arab dress called and whistled to one another as panniers of mangoes and bananas were unloaded from the large wooden dhows creaking at the jetty. Others enquired anxiously about leaving times and destinations as they stepped over obstructions on deck, peering around crumpled sails and rough hewn masts. Small lean donkeys laden with water and building materials wandered between heaps of sand and piles of 'bricks' cut from coral rock, disappearing with their owners up the narrow lanes that ran at right angles to the wharf.

We followed them, immediately struck by the cool air and foetid smells of these tall sunless alleys. Flea ridden cats licked their wounds in dank doorways and effluent ran in open gutters, making its way slowly to the sea. Men walked soundlessly on sandaled feet and women, modestly covered from head to toe, flashed winsome glances with knowing eyes. Even today, our guide told us, male visitors are not allowed inside another man's house. Only the women may enter.

A glimpse into the airy light filled rooms and inner courtyards of the houses belied their unwelcoming exterior. The men, we were told, will be served coffee outside, seated in the alcove at the entrance to each home.

Only the frequent interruptions of our guide's mobile phone reminded us that we had not stepped backwards into a time warp. It still seemed unreal, perhaps as if we were on location, on a film-set somewhere. One thing was certain: The mosque, now as it was then, is the focus of all their lives; the call to prayer eagerly obeyed. Our tour ended in the Museum where the enthusiasm of our guide made ample compensation for the minimal exhibits. Lamu, like the other coastal islands of Zanzibar and Madagascar was built on trade with the Arabs. They brought brass and silver, spices and Islam to Kenya and took away timber, copra, coconut oil, foodstuffs – and slaves.

Feeling somewhat faint and grimy from the odoriferous heat, and knowing that we were going to the stylish Peponi's Hotel for lunch, I thought I would have to be brave and use the toilet facilities in the Museum to freshen myself up. I knew it would be ghastly, but the desire to at least wash my hands overcame my reticence.

It WAS ghastly: dark and very smelly. I advanced towards the basin, waiting for my eyes to adjust to the gloom. I washed my hands under the tap and wondered if I could be brave enough to use the drain in the floor that served as a toilet. It would mean closing the door and being in total darkness. I hesitated, then swung the door half closed. I don't know who was more shocked. Me or... the rat! We stared momentarily at one another, pink eyed in the gloom, weighing our chances. He was very large – and very wet, having presumably crawled up the drain I was about to use. I did not wait to see his reaction. I retreated with all haste, in some disarray.

'There's a rat! There's a rat!' I yelled at our guide.

He was unmoved by my discovery:

'Ah!' he said, somewhat profoundly 'A rat. That is Africa.'

44

July 2004

Sunshine and storms

━━◦◉◦━━

Spring ended on a sad note: We had to call the vet to our darling girl Flossie, our sheepdog and dearest companion for thirteen years. Kindly, he gave her an injection where she had collapsed on the lawn and in a sudden flurry of falling cherry blossom she was gone, leaving us bereft.

In need of solace we left our home and remaining livestock in the capable hands of friends and set off on our travels. May became a month of castles and car journeys, changing scenery and changeable weather. Through sunshine and storms we drove through the wild garlic and blue-bells of the lanes here in the South West, through middle England where the roads were laced with the pink and white confections of hawthorn hedges and flowering horse chestnuts trees, to our friends in the flatlands of East Anglia and the marshes beyond. Then, in June, we swapped lush green English countryside for hot sunshine and the golden cornfields of Northern France to stay with friends and attend a nephew's wedding.

Our first stop was Caerhayes Castle opposite Porthluny Beach in Cornwall. Swathed in a damp sea mist we marvelled at the ancient camellias, magnolia and rhododendrons; towering mountains of colour against a backdrop of ancient woodland. Their head gardener enthused about the Williamsii hybrids created by the castle's owners and explained the devastation of the damage limitation imposed on them by D.E.F.R.A. to restrict the spread of 'Sudden Oak Death. The virus affects the American oaks in particular, but also rhododendrons, camellias and other acid loving plants. We sympathised with his dilemma. With no absolute proof that it will be effective in curbing the disease, to cut out and burn historic shrubs on this scale is a heartbreaking task. What about all the rhododendrons that grow wild in neighbouring woodland, or along the railway embankments? Are they all to be weeded out too?

At Sherbourne Castle in Dorset it was the 'house' rather than the gardens that merited attention: In particular, for me, the library. It is a relatively small gem of a room, in the ornate Gothick (neo-Gothic) style of Strawberry Hill. How lovely it would have been to take a leather-bound tome from the shelves and while away the afternoon there, looking up occasionally to glance across the lawns and watch a flight of duck home in on the lake beyond.

At Framlingham Castle in Suffolk all signs of former comfort had long since disappeared, leaving only the circular curtain of its outer wall and its ornate chimney stacks intact. I was already dizzy by the time I had climbed the narrow circular stairway to the top of the tower. The ensuing walk around the ramparts made me so giddy I was quite unable to admire the 'superb view' advertised in the brochure, concentrating instead on placing one foot firmly in front of the other. Seeing a man poised to launch himself over the side of the castellated wall, for a moment I thought he too might be suffering from a bout of vertigo:

'Are you OK?' I asked, just as he disappeared from view. White knuckled, I forced myself to peer over the edge. He grinned up at me as he abseiled casually down the outside of the castle wall.

'Do you do this for pleasure?' I asked, feeling my head begin to swim.

'No,' he replied cheerily, 'I'm a surveyor checking for cracks in the masonry.'

Thinking that if I looked down any longer I might land on top of him I withdrew, hauling myself hand over hand along the safety rail to the exit.

In Suffolk, in brilliant sunshine, we enjoyed the tranquillity of Snape Maltings, the waterside setting for the Aldburgh Music festival. In Aldburgh we liked the Medieval Moot House and the controversial modern sculpture of Shells on the beach. In Southwold we walked to the end of the Pier and thought how grey and uninviting the North Sea looks after our sunny Salcombe blue.

Without the rising contours of our Devon hills the East Anglian skies seem vast and the horizons endless. In Norfolk we could appreciate the special light that inspires so many artists to go there and paint. Its clarity gives definition to busy coastal scenes and lonely windswept beaches. At times the sky seemed filled with far too many clouds, like shoals of big grey fish swimming across an ocean of blue, the land below reduced to an insignificant streak of yellow or green.

In Lincolnshire heavy showers of rain brought relief to gardeners and farmers alike. Its flat acres of Grade 1 soil make it a powerhouse of productivity. Vast fields of potatoes and sugar beet stretch as far as the eye can see as our English producers battle to beat off foreign competition. Already most of the traditional onion growers have ceased production, using their extensive (and expensive) climate-controlled storage sheds to store onions from Chile instead. Now the concern is for the future of the sugar beet growers as the EU is pressurised to import more cane sugar from under-developed countries. It is easy to see how world economics affect not only our industry but also our landscape. In France we again felt anxious for our British farmers as we drove for hours through seemingly endless hectares of high yielding wheat and barley, marvelling at both its quality and quantity.

The wedding was a three day event requiring stamina and dedication. Our noisy motorcade of klaxoning cars was led by the bride and groom in a lime green Cadillac covered with bouquets so large they could easily have graced the hearse of a gangland funeral. There were strict words from the Mayor at the Civil Ceremony about the couple's responsibility to each other and to any future children, then handfuls of rose petals after betrothals and blessings from the Priest in an ancient Catholic church. Amidst laughter and smiles a tireless photographer took zillions and squillions of photographs ensuring that the entire congregation arrived at the reception with a sizeable thirst and an unlimited desire to offer alcoholic toasts to the bride and groom throughout the proceedings. Food, wine, conversation and music flowed throughout the night with grandmothers and great aunts dancing through the small hours. A brief respite for breakfast and a change of clothes and then it was time to begin again with another six course luncheon the following day. The generous hospitality and lack of sleep meant that the rest of our stay passed in an amiable blur of bonhomie, further strengthening the 'entente cordiale' that has bound our two families together for so long – ever since Mireille and my older sister Georgina began corresponding as schoolgirl penpals nearly 40 years ago!!

Returning at last to Horswell we weave our way up the drive avoiding branches and debris littered by passing storms. Ducks doze on the lawn surrounded by twigs and fallen leaves and a young fox looks back at us over his shoulder as he stoops to drink at the pond. Startled by our arrival he springs into nearby bushes within inches of our remaining three Guinea Fowl. They turn to chase him, cackling angrily, oblivious to their own danger. Hearing the commotion Bertie gallops towards us, his tail beating circles in the air, stirring a trail of happiness in his wake.

We step from the car and breathe in the scent of full blown roses mingled with fresh salt laden air. Mmmm! Mon Dieu, it is good to be home! Even without our darling Flossie to greet us.

45

Chaos in the House!

———◦◦◦———

It was love at first sight. I who had thought I could never feel that way again and he, so sure that he wanted to be mine that he left his family and the only home he had ever known without a backward glance. Briefly I had held his chin in the palm of my hand, tilting his face towards mine. 'If I take you home with me, will you...' I asked, 'Will you always be my very special friend?'

'Yesssss!' he seemed to reply, returning my gaze with unwavering certainty. And since that moment I have only to whisper his name and he is beside me, his warmth comforting and secure as he presses his body against mine.

His name is Jack and he is our new 4 month old black Labrador puppy. As I write he is stretched out at my feet, his coat gleaming like molten tar in the sunshine. Such is the intensity of our relationship that my husband no longer answers to the call of 'Darling?' lest he should be offered a Bonio. Meanwhile Bertie the Briard prowls around us, an archetype of brooding menace. Stiff legged and resentful he ignores my offers of love and friendship, preferring to regard our new arrival with wolfish yellow eyes, plotting his revenge.

Hoping to redress the balance, two weeks later we collected a small female bundle of black and white fur, as soft and weightless as a powder

153

puff. We called her Milly and watched with pleasure as Bertie's body language softened into happy acceptance. At last he understood that he was not being replaced but was again going to have a Labrador and a Border Collie to play with; friends to bolster his courage and comfort him when loud bangs or exploding fireworks turn him into a quivering jelly.

Four weeks into our affair and Jack and I still steal glances like covert lovers behind the others' backs, but with Milly to play with, Bertie to pacify and Horswell to explore our quiet moments together are few and far between. His days are filled with eating, sleeping, playing tag across the lawn and hide and seek through the bushes. Or alternatively: up-ending all my plant pots, stealing tools and timber from the builders as they work and CHEWING !!! Aided and abetted by Milly, Jack has turned our Kitchen and Breakfast Room into a war zone. Upholstered chairs have been gutted, their stuffing strewn around the room like feathers after a fox's rampage through a chicken house. Wallpaper and plaster have been ripped from the walls and every corner of skirting board and kitchen unit has been chewed to a soggy pulp. I had quite forgotten what damage two puppies in 'destruct mode' can inflict – and soooo quickly!

Discipline must of necessity be enforced, but the sight of two tiny heads and two pairs of eyes peering anxiously around a corner, is maddeningly disarming. Of course I still thunder and growl but my admiration for Jack (who allows Milly to run and hide while he comes forward to take the blame) is such that, after we have agreed that it was a 'Very Bad Thing To Do', I end up heaping praise on his courage and allowing him to creep onto my lap in meek submission. They say love is blind. It is also jolly expensive!

Other 'Very Bad Things To Do' have included stealing the builder's mobile phone and burying it in the rose garden, chewing our phone and in the process dialling 999 (Well, actually, 9999990000000***//, but luckily not 'Go') and digging a 'Very Big Hole' in the middle of the croquet lawn. So large and so deep was the offending hole that for a moment we wondered if my father who is due to arrive by Quantas from Australia might have discovered an alternative way of travel.

Whilst Milly's little earth covered snout peered out from under a nearby bush, Jack listened politely to my anti-digging monologue. He cocked his head on one side intelligently, weighed my argument carefully

154

and waited (for some time) for me to finish. By way of reply he dived head first into the crater and re-appeared with a recently dispatched mole clenched firmly between his teeth – thus simultaneously succeeding in nailing the pest who had been wrecking our lawns for some time, and demolishing all my theories on suitable canine behaviour.

Aware of a relaxation in the tension in dog/human relationships Milly then re-appeared onto the scene, sniffing the grass with her pointy little nose to tell me that it was she who had actually scented the mole and marked the exact spot for Jack to dig, and that contrary to my initial assumption she was in fact 'A Very Good Girl Indeed.'

Certainly Milly does have a very good 'nose' and has already proved herself to be a fearless huntress. Rather like our guinea fowl (who were spotted pursuing a fox across the ley apparently regardless of their own danger), Milly flushed a young fox from his lair in the rhododendron bush by the house, sending it at full stretch past our tea-party on the lawn, startling us all. By the size of him, Milly would have made no more than a tasty morsel if the roles had been reversed! Anyone who condemns the hunting of foxes with dogs is ignoring this very simple fact of nature. A fox has far more chance of escape or a speedy end from a dog than from a misplaced bullet fired on an alcohol fuelled 'lamping' expedition.

With regard to fox-hunting, what disgraceful scenes of violence were witnessed outside Westminster recently. Which other minority group would be treated with such brute force and icy contempt? Had it been the face of an ethnic minority shown beaten and bleeding from a policeman's truncheon rather than that of a country woman hoping to defend her traditional English way of life, the country would have been in uproar. And did you see the mere handful of MPs taking part in the debate in the Commons? An historic debate that threatens to change a way of life pursued for centuries in this country? I say let country men and women decide the ways of the countryside not urban politicians who hide behind their barricades and baton wielding police force.

Sadly the skirmishes within the House as bailiffs attempted to evict the young pro-hunt supporters will be used to distance the Government even further from the people it should be representing. Tightened security will mean less Public access to the Commons and probably the end of the right to demonstrate within a bomb's throw of Parliament Square. It is the tightening of the screw. Unless we are vigilant the political agenda of our rulers will destroy the liberty and freedom of speech we have until now believed to be the basis of our democracy.

Thank God for the sanctuary of Horswellia! For the dogs and the ducks and the birds, for the storm tossed woods and the golden autumnal days. For air so crisp and clean it revives one's spirits like champagne sipped from a crystal flute. For sunshine dappling through pale green discs of beech and lime, and the scent of roses mixed with musky, leaf-strewn earth. For our new gazebo with its views through trees to the fountain beyond. Thank God for all the lovely visitors who have filled our home all summer. But above all, thank you now for the time to be here alone with our little family to savour its beauty and its peace.

46

CHRISTMAS 2004

A time to remember...

————◦◦◦————

November, a month of windswept skies and flaming sunsets, of pungent wood-smoke and golden leaves; fireworks, dog walks and short damp days. A time of bitter-sweet reunion and harsh remembrance.

82 years old and suffering from severe shingles my father made the long journey to England from Queensland, Australia, and thankfully, despite the presence of a two year old child with ear ache in the adjoining seat, he survived the experience. Earlier in the year we had wondered if we should ever see him again so it was with a mixture of joy and relief that I collected him from Heathrow. Confident that the Horswell magic would soon work its charm on his ailing health we hurried down the motorway as fast as the speed cameras would allow, to bring him home for food and rest.

His reason for coming was two fold: To see his publisher before the launch of his book ('Focus on Europe – A Photo-Reconnaissance Mosquito pilot at war, 1943-45') and to attend the final reunion of the Mosquito Aircrew Association. Well, I suppose there might have been another reason too: To see my mother, perhaps one last time, knowing she also has suffered ill health of late.

In the days that followed his arrival we slowly built bridges across the years that we had been apart. As we journeyed around the countryside I concentrated on the driving while he, like a taut spring unravelling, unleashed the loneliness that had dogged him in recent months. He talked to me constantly, like a computer downloading, emptying the 'files' that had been stored for years so meticulously in his brain. Writing his memoirs had opened old wounds and brought thoughts and feelings, long buried, bubbling back to the surface.

The accuracy of his recall was phenomenal, each event, each attack, each manoeuvre remembered in striking detail. As we swooped down the motorways or wound our way through country villages I was transported by his accounts to the great blue yonder above the clouds. As I scanned the horizon for police cars and speed traps I marvelled at the lonely courage of a twenty three year old Kiwi boy and his English navigator, my godfather Frank Moseley, unarmed and reliant solely on their flying skills and the speed and flexibility of their sky-blue Mosquito to outwit the Focke-Wulf 190's sent to prevent them taking their reconnaissance photos and to shoot them down.

Ron, my father, is the last remaining pilot of his squadron. At the final reunion of the Mosquito Aircrew Association the only man he knew was 'Ginger' Baylis, an observer/navigator. They had never flown together, but the bond when they met was instant and immeasurable. Looking around the room that first evening I thought that we were just like any other crowd; ordinary, unremarkable. But my thoughts would change as the weekend progressed.

The following day a reception was held for us at the Hendon Aircraft Museum. Expecting that we would be standing about in draughty hangars with oil-stained floors I swathed myself in a warm coat and layers of clothes. I need not have bothered. The Museum is modern and light, the aircraft all lovingly polished and in mint condition. Our party hurried single-mindedly through the exhibits towards the Mosquito on display, their affection, admiration and pride in the aircraft clearly written on their faces.

The Mosquito was the wrong colour and build for Photo Reconnaissance. The camera pods had been extended to carry a heavy payload of bombs and the airframe was marked with the black and white stripes that identified it as part of the D-day Allied Invasion. Men huddled in small groups beneath its outstretched wings, each recalling in their different ways the love and respect that they shared for a magnificent flying machine that, often against all the odds, had brought them home and saved their lives.

That evening, at the formal dinner, I looked around and saw a different crowd of men. Imbued with the camaraderie of shared experiences and fired by the enduring spirit of the indomitable Mossie, these men seemed to walk taller, to hold their spines straighter, their chins higher. Where before I had seen only ordinariness, now I realised I was in the presence of an elite force. These men, in their youth, would have been like young gods; handsome and courageous, taking to the sky in the fastest, sexiest aircraft of their day. Time and again they had stared death in the face, prepared to lay down their lives for the freedom of the country they loved; each and every one of them a hero worthy of our gratitude and respect. What a priviledge it was to meet them! I felt honoured to be in such distinguished company and humbled by their greatness. Like a child, walking in the footsteps of giants.

As the National Anthem was played at the end of the final commemorative church service there were no tears but plenty of stiff upper lips and ramrod straight backs. I could not sing a note. The sight of such dedication to Queen and Country whilst our politicians and post war generations squander our sovereignty and fritter away the freedoms these men had fought for, was too much to bear. Overwhelmed by the intense emotion of the day we beat a hasty retreat, blaming the incense for the moisture in our eyes and the sudden chill in the air for our hasty search for handkerchiefs.

On our way back to the airport at Heathrow for my father's return flight we stopped in Oxfordshire to take my mother out for lunch. We drove to a favourite haunt, The Beetle and Wedge by the river at Moulsford. We sat at a table by the window and watched pleasure boats and skiffs pass by, and cows grazing in the meadow beyond. The afternoon seemed to spin away from us leaving us in a cosy vacuum where time stood still. As the meal progressed past memories entwined with the day's pleasures. Where there had been gaps and bottomless black holes in our family history we found enough threads to weave our lives back together and pull it into shape. It was the first time I had seen my parents together in over 40 years and watching them laugh and chatter, relaxed and easy in each other's company I thought my heart would burst. I had to leave the table and made the excuse of paying the bill.

'Don't be such a Pollyanna' my friends had said when, all those years ago, my parents had divorced. 'Don't waste your time and emotions hoping that they will ever get back together. That's not real life.'

'But they love each other.' I used to say. 'They are meant to be together. Even if they cannot live together, they should just be best friends.'

'Oh, doooo grow up.' They used to reply. 'Don't be such a Pollyana. Life doesn't always have happy endings.'

As I signed my credit card slip I glanced back at our table. Autumn sunshine slanted through the window, warm and golden. I watched as my father leant forward to say something and saw the faint blush that rose in my mother's cheeks. She said something to him in reply, her eyes big and blue and dancing with laughter, and he laughed too. They made a handsome couple, totally absorbed in each other's company. If I hadn't known them, I would have said they were in love.

47

JANUARY 2005

'For whom the bell tolls...'

———◦◦◦———

Is it simply that an indulgent Christmas has expanded our girth or is it the world around us that has suddenly shrunk and become very small ? These days News travels at the speed of light, privacy and isolation appear to have no meaning and self sufficiency seems to be as redundant as a dinosaur. Suddenly we are all world citizens and there is nowhere to hide. Whether it is the television or the tax man, the telephone, the computer, the charity fund raiser or the hard-nosed salesman we are never it seems allowed to be 'incommunicado'. Was it the events of 9/11 that gave us the by-word 24/7? Wherever it came from, its meaning seems to have infil-trated our lives. Availability and accessibility 24 hours a day, 7 days a week.

Never before has John Donne's epithet 'No man is an island' seemed more true: Modern technology and communications meant that the hideous destruction of the Asian tsunami reached us with eyewitness immediacy. Within hours images of horror and mayhem captured by amateur photographers fighting for their lives brought the full force of the tidal wave crashing into homes around the world, uniting us all in an international reaction of shock and disbelief.

John Donne also wrote: 'Any man's death diminishes me, because I am involved in mankind. And therefore never send to know for whom the bell tolls; it tolls for thee' We are all global neighbours now. Or is that global voyeurs? How can we not feel involved when we have witnessed with such intrusive candour so much suffering and grief? For those of us lucky enough to have spent time in the countries affected by the tsunami, for those who have enjoyed the exotic beauty of the scenery and the gentle charm of the people, the sight of such devastation can only reinforce our desire and responsibility to offer assistance. For everyone, everywhere, the appalling loss of so many lives must surely be a reason to offer thanks for one's own existence and the safety of all those who have been spared.

For a short while at least tragedy has united us, allowing us to forget our petty squabbles. We dig deep into our pockets to fund humanitarian aid while our politicians make fine speeches and strive to match our generosity. We are all world citizens now. In touch with our finer feelings and our fellow men. Goodness is triumphing over adversity and Life, because it no longer seems a certainty, has regained its value. Hooray!

But with such accessibility and ease of communication can there ever be a feeling of peace? Now that the world has shrunk it seems to revolve even faster, making life crazier by the day. For example:

- In Oxfordshire recently I was questioned by a stranger about something my husband and I had discussed privately in Devon two days earlier. A friend – of a friend – of a friend – had provided the link. On the golf links, as it happens! No need for a carrier pigeon when companions are so efficient.

- Thanks to the World Wide Web, as I sit here and write I can see via my laptop, a pod of Bryde whales swimming alongside my sister's yacht as she sails off the New Zealand coast between Great Barrier and Coromandel.

- If the telephone rings I am either asked to take part in a survey or invited to claim a prize by someone so foreign as to be unintelligible. And if I ask for assistance or call Directory Enquiries my request is routed via Outer Mongolia to India. Our conversation is then conducted in some strange incomprehensible mixture of Alpha, Bravo, Charlie, Delta accented with Hindi-American overtones.

- At the supermarket we purchase produce from Chile, Kenya and Peru; in the garden we enjoy bulbs from Holland and in the driveway today are vehicles from Germany, Italy and Sweden.

- Friends holidaying abroad bombard us with postcards bearing the inane (but welcome) utterings of brains idling in neutral. For example: 'Velly Melly Clistmas' (from China) or 'Would you like us to p-p-pick up a penguin?' (from the Galapagos) Does their choice of destination simply demonstrate how far people will travel for a two week vacation? Or how small the world has become?

- In the newspapers we eagerly follow Ellen MacArthur's progress as she attempts to circumnavigate the world on her 75' Trimaran in less than the existing record of 72 days, 22 hours, 54 minutes and 22 seconds. When seconds enter the equation of long distance records you *know* the world has become small!!

We are, it would appear, all members of a Global Village, whether we like it or not and with photographs from Titan, (one of the moons orbiting Saturn), travelling 750million miles to reach earth in under 70 minutes, this is just the beginning.

It surely cannot be long before we are exchanging holiday snaps not only with people on the other side of the world, but with our neighbours from outer space.

Meanwhile here at Horswell, even in the rain, the garden looks lovely, with water cascading into the pond and skeletal trees etched spider-black against a storm-lit sky. Snowdrops, aconites and primroses are already in flower and the ravens are croaking as they return to inspect last year's nests. A cymbidium orchid left outside in the courtyard has four healthy flower spikes pushing up through its long strappy leaves and the grape vine nearby is in bud, testimony to the mild winter we have had so far.

Every year it is exciting to watch the garden coming to life; each emerging bud and shoot a welcome harbinger of spring. If one looks carefully there is always beauty to be found, whatever the weather. I know I have used this quotation before but, after all the uncertainty and grim tragedy of the tsunami these words of Walter de la Mare seem particularly relevant now:

'Look thy last on all things lovely every hour. Let no night seal thy sense in deathly slumber, 'till to delight thou have paid thy utmost blessing.' In other words, we must take nothing for granted, fully appreciate all that we have and know that it is precious. For tomorrow it may not be there. On that cheerful note, I think I'll go and give the dogs another goodnight kiss!

48

MARCH 2005

Three pairs of ears

———◦◉◦———

Three pairs of ears register the 'click' as I silence the roar of the vacuum cleaner with a flick of a switch. Three pairs of eyes, bright with expectation, watch intently as the fire breathing dragon with its lead now tightly coiled is dragged, docile and compliant, across the room. Three pointy noses turn to watch as the monster is bundled into the cupboard, its serpent's neck wrapped hideously around a long metallic leg. Three furry heads nod their approval as I close the door, 12 padded feet dancing a fandango of suppressed excitement. 'Has she?' (finished the housework) 'Is she?' (going to take us out) 'Are we?' (going out, at last) Their questions pierce my defences with their persistence.

I reach for my wellies. Three tails thunder in syncopated rhythm: Boom-Boom-Boom on the Dresser, Bang-Bang-Bang against the chair, Ting-a-ling-a-ling on the door of the washing machine. Thumpety-thumpety- thump-thump-thump on the table leg, Ding-ding-ding on the dog's bowl and a cymbal crash as a basket of jam jars hits the floor.

As I bend to slide each foot inside a boot, paws and claws scrabble at my back showering me with encouragement. 'Yes! Yes!' They say. 'Well done! You're doing the right thing!'

A moment's hesitation as I survey the coat rack, and tails hang still and silent. Six anxious eyes dart fleetingly between the green coat that I

165

wear for gardening and the brown tweed hacking jacket that I wear for walking. Three anxious dogs try to second guess my next move, worried that I'll make the wrong decision. A surge of enthusiasm as I brush past the tweed coat to reach for my scarf. A quick drumroll, swiftly silenced, as I seem to head towards the secateurs and shears. I look in the mirror and arrange my scarf. Three pairs of eyes swivel back to the coat rack. An eternity of waiting. And then they know. A crescendo of barking and wagging and thumping and banging as I take the tweed jacket from its hanger and put it on. 'She did it!' they say 'She took the right one!'

I reach for their leads and slip them like a noose around my neck as dogs race wildly around the room falling over one another with excitement. I stuff my pockets with polythene bags and take my stick. 'It's a walk! A walk! A WALK!' they bark, loud enough to inform the entire neighbourhood. And off we go.

Jack and Milly tear off across the lawn frightening grazing ducks back onto the pond whilst big Bertie lumbers after them, his tail stirring the air like a starting handle. The three guinea fowl hurry out of the way gobbling and grumbling like small turkeys whereas the peacocks continue pecking for grubs, determined to stand their ground.

At the pond Jack the Labrador is leaning out across the water, hoping for an excuse to fall in. His mind is focussed on retrieving one of the startled ducks, the concepts of 'tame' and 'pet' being hard for a hunting dog to understand. Luckily Milly distracts him and they rush off together through the trees, their noses hoovering up the trail of a badger. Further down the driveway they reappear, crashing through the bushes and trampling daffodils underfoot. I notice that the aconites have gone now and that the snowdrops were short-lived this year. Primroses are taking their place, spreading their broad green leaves above the carpet of winter moss and twiggery. Cold winds and frosts have browned all the early camellias this year, but later blooms make vibrant splashes of colour that look extravagant and exotic against our wintry browns and greens.

Puppy drill means that we stop at the gate and listen hard for traffic, look right and left and right again and then it's a mad free-for-all as we dash across the road and run full tilt along and down the footpath, over (or under) the stile and down across the field to the stream at the bottom. The field has recently been ploughed, the sharp cut of the ploughshare clearly visible where it has gouged the blood red soil from its slumber and turned it upside down. Away in the distance the sea glints in the cold sunlight, a silver lining to the grey cloud where the coastline fades from Devon into Cornwall.

Across the valley sheep are grazing, seemingly oblivious to the cold and biting wind. They remind me of my own initiation into the delights of sheep farming many years ago when I married my husband. I returned to England in March, leaving behind my Sydney lifestyle and a stifling Australian summer.

It was bitterly cold in Oxfordshire, with snow on the ground and ice solid in the water buckets and glistening in the tractor tracks. I arrived at night, and was informed that I was in time to do the midnight to 4.a.m. night watch!

Swathed in layers of jumpers and scarves and a pair of 'Uncle Bill's long johns that he had worn at Gallipoli' – complete with bullet holes. Or was it the moth? – I was probably too trussed up to be much use but I found the whole process of the birth and ensuring that the new born lambs were bonding with their mothers and suckling properly almost mystical in its simplicity. I treasure the memory of that first night in England although when I look at the photograph of the suntanned woman taken by my friend at Sydney Airport and the photograph taken outside the farmhouse 48 hours later I can hardly believe that it is the same person. Me.

Our walk to the beach means careful corralling of the dogs along the busy Thurlestone road. They know that, although usually silent, when I speak it is because there is something they need to know. 'Car, car, car!' may sound like a wounded crow but thankfully it has the desired effect as cars whoosh by at speed.Drivers seem evenly divided between those who slow for animals and those who press on regardless. The closer we get to the beach the faster our progress, until, as we round the final corner, the desire for puppies to be puppies is simply too great and the descent to the beach becomes a helter-skelter rush of noise and enthusiasm.

There are few pleasures as cathartic as throwing a stick and watching the excitement of dogs hurling themselves into the water to retrieve it. My arm may ache with the repeated effort but the joy released by this simple action is always worth it: The look of concentration on their faces, the competitive positioning and game-plan, the eager anticipation.

And then the sudden turn of speed, the race, the search, the determination to succeed. After that comes the serious debate about who actually picked the stick from the water, the tussle and the tiff, the growls and the grumbles, the need for praise and arbitration. And above all, a new throw and a new excuse to plunge back into the waves. The difficulty only comes in persuading them that the game, eventually, is over and it is time to leave.

The walk home is a rambling uncoordinated affair. With fewer cars on the South Milton Road there is time to push noses down rabbit holes, startle blackbirds from the hedgerows and savour interesting smells. As Jack and Milly scamper ahead, Bertie and I make our way steadily behind them enjoying our few moments together without intrusion from the younger dogs. We amble along contentedly side by side, silent except for the tap tap tap of my stick and the click click click of his long claws on the road. We do not really know how old Bertie is but certainly his coat is very grey these days. With age has come a sweetness of temperament and a wisdom and patience that he lacked when he was younger. They say you cannot teach an old dog new tricks. But maybe we can all learn new tricks from an old dog.

49

MAY 2005

Matriarch of the Pacific

At school my Geography teacher was describing the fruits grown in a temperate Mediterranean climate. I can remember the sounds of her words now as clearly as if it were yesterday: 'Plums, peaches, grapes, cherries and apricots.' The fruits seemed to drip from her lips like juice from an over-ripe melon. They sounded plump and sweet, succulent, and sensuous. I could taste their honey, lick the bloom from their skin, feel the warmth of the sunshine in which they grew. I knew immediately that I must travel, to go to such a place and sense its delights for myself.

You could hear our French mistress long before she entered the class-room. Her high sling-back heels clacked merrily along the corridor as she approached. On a waft of perfume she would swirl into the room, a medley of colour; a bright figure-hugging dress, bare brown arms and legs, a generous mouth dashed with lipstick the colour of nectarines. 'Bonjour, mes enfants!' she would call out gaily as she dumped a pile of homework onto a table by the door. 'Bonjour Madame!' we sang in chorus as she perched on the edge of her desk, crossing one suntanned leg over the other and letting her shoe hang wickedly loose from the tip of an outstretched toe. Against the dull bookishness of the other teachers, who fluttered through the door like grey sparrows in their gowns she seemed a rare and exotic bird. I knew from the start of that first lesson that learning French was going to be a pleasure and that France was the place for me.

Driving through the cherry blossom and vineyards of the Var and the Vaucluse last month, with the sunshine warm on my skin and the sky blue and clear above snow capped mountains I thought of the immense influence those two women have had on my life. They sowed seeds in my fertile imagination, seeds that have grown and grown through the years and whose rich harvest I continue to reap. I wish they were still alive so that I could say thank you.

I thought of them again the other day at the Kingsbridge Community College where my husband and I were privileged to present the Horswell Cup to a young lady with a prodigious musical talent. It was part of an evening of celebration; of displays and recitals and the distribution of awards. For us it was an evening of pure delight. The atmosphere was one of genuine affection and mutual respect between pupils and staff. The children were happy and self confident and the standard of teaching and facilities available to them seemed quite exceptional. Sitting there amongst them, watching and listening, I wondered if those students would, like me, one day remember the teacher who gave them the inspiration to excel at their chosen subject and want to come back and honour them for enriching their lives?

For those members of staff handing out their awards that evening were more than mere mortals. They were the gatekeepers to knowledge. They may be unable to accompany every child on its unique journey through life, but they can push open the doors to discovery, prising them open just wide enough to allow a tantalising glimpse of the possibilities that lie beyond. They can light fires in a child's imagination and give them the tools and the map to pursue their dreams. And who could ask for a more valuable gift?

Talking of valuable gifts I received an early birthday present from my sister this morning. I think the brightly coloured stamps emblazoned with 'Merry Christmas from the Kingdom of Tonga' were almost as attractive as the shell bracelet enveloped beneath them. (I don't suppose an enormous amount of mail emanates from the island of Tonga Tapu hence the unseasonal greeting.) This may appear a simple gift but it is worth its weight in pure gold. Why? Because it proves that my sister has survived her first long sea passage on her yacht Caesura, the first leg of a long held ambition to sail from New Zealand around the world. No small feat for an occasional weekend sailor. (Inspired by her Geography teacher perhaps ??) The accompanying Birthday card bears a painting of a deliciously curvaceous island woman lazing on a hot yellow beach beside a turquoise sea, eating ripe mangoes and wearing frangipani flowers braided in her hair. On the reverse side the artist states rather grandly: 'I choose to paint women, the Matriarchs of the Pacific, expressing their gentle dignity and serenity. If I have achieved my goal the viewer will feel an emotional attachment to my subjects.' Sitting here by the heater, swathed in Damart and eyeing a decidedly grey and unalluring sky outside, let me tell you dear reader: The artist has failed.

Is Summer ever going to arrive? Or am I going to spend my Birthday coughing and wheezing my way through the latest cold? Red-eyed and rheumy, clutching a hot-toddy (That's a drink, by the way) and cuddled up to the Aga?

Why the delay? Where's that heat-wave they have been promising? You know, the one with the water shortage attached? What about global warming? I want it. Now!

It is even hard to be enthusiastic about gardening when the ground is sodden and the lawns too wet to mow. As the daffodils die back the weeds grow higher, the box hedging straggles out of shape and goose-grass grows apace stretching out its barbed tentacles to smother all that lies beneath. Beside the pond a grass snake slumbers beneath broad leaves; cool and damp, half seen in dappled light. The cuckoo calls once, then twice, then seems to hesitate perhaps to question if he has the season right. Despite the chill the swallows have returned, flickering and twisting through the air, transporting mud to build their nests. At dusk the bats emerge from holes and cracks to sweep the skies for airborne gnats. At night a vixen howls calling her young to share her feed. Next morning a sad trail of black and white spotted feathers shows that it is one of our Guinea fowl that has given them their evening meal.

Beyond our walls the hedgerows froth and overflow with sudden growth. As grass overtakes the bluebells, cow parsley and campion conspire to hide burgeoning docks and nettles while purple orchids fade and disappear. As we pass through the lanes winds scatter the passing hours of dandelion clocks and young green ferns extend their ladders towards the sky. Further north, driving through the Cotswolds with my mother, horse chestnut trees sag beneath their weight of flowers, black and white cows graze in buttercup meadows, and fields of yellow rape flash neon bright against dark rain-swelled skies.

Home again and the chaos of workmen and the smell of new paint fill the house. In the library the white woodwork is gleaming and the yellow walls are brighter than before. In fact... quite a lot brighter. Seriously bright. I'm talking sunglasses here! But hold on, don't panic... I check the label on the paint tin. Californian Sands. Perfect! All I need now is a beach towel, a sarong and flowers in my hair to escape the winter blues and get in touch with my 'Matriarch of the Pacific' dignity and calm.

Aloha!

50

AUGUST 2005

Wallpaper madness

——◦◦◦——

It's been a crazy few weeks: The decorators are still here. After three months I'm beginning to feel like a sparrow with a family of cuckoos disrupting my nest. Indeed bird-brained would be a good way of describing my state of mind recently. Take the wallpaper problem for instance: We have all seen it, we all agree that the vital roll to complete the downstairs corridor is here in the house somewhere, we are all SURE we can find it. But the truth is: we can't. Meanwhile Darty and I camp out in the kitchen sitting on hard garden chairs because:

a.) The upholsterer has had our proper chairs for so long I would not recognise them if they appeared on Crimewatch.

b.) With the corridor half finished the effort to reach any other part of the house necessitates an expedition to the South Pole and back via several flights of stairs and wanderings through bedrooms various. By which time encroaching senility assures that we have forgotten why we set off in the first place and ensures that whatever we meant to bring with us has been left behind!

We have searched high and low in every conceivable nook and cranny for the missing paper; behind bookcases, on top of wardrobes, in dark corners of damp cellars, toolsheds, garages and bat-infested attic hideaways. All to no avail. And then we searched all over again. And then again. Despite a clear picture in our minds of exactly how the roll of paper is lying (Next to another scrap of the same wallpaper, covered in thick dust) we have had no success and nearly driven ourselves insane in the search. Did I say nearly?? I wonder sometimes...

In desperation I called the local clairvoyant for a consultation. 'Is there something specific that you want to discuss?' she asked 'What exactly is the problem?' I do not know how far up the scale of eccentricity 'I've lost the wallpaper' comes but seemingly unfazed by my request she agreed to bring her pendulum and help us look.

My husband is, of necessity, a long suffering man. But when Abigail greeted him with a shocked 'It's YOU !! I've been looking for you for so long. Don't you remember me? La Rochelle 1640. I brought all my horses. You sailed without me!' and later failed dismally to locate the missing wallpaper I think he began to wonder who out of the three of us had lost what? (The strange thing is that they really did seem to recognise each other and my husband has always had a soft spot for La Rochelle!)

After Abigail had left I felt a strong urge to go and look in my wardrobe. Sure enough I found a roll of wallpaper. But maddeningly the wrong one! It reminded me of the conversation we had had: She told how she had worked for the police in locating a missing person. When they dug up the site she had 'visualised' they found bones. But not the bones of the missing person. The bones of a corpse from a different century!!!!

So after all our efforts the decorators could not progress and the only piece of wallpaper in our possession was the one scrap that Jack and Milly had ripped from the wall without chewing it into a million bits. We were guarding it with our life.

Our search had highlighted the vast amount of clutter we seem to have collected in our 14 years at Horswell. I say 'we' to keep the peace. What I really mean is that my husband is a hoarder. In the cellar I found all manner of junk that I KNOW I had previously asked him to remove from the toolshed, and in the toolshed I discovered a whole lot of rubbish previously housed in the cellar! Under severe duress a skip was hired. Determined to get full value for money we started early. I donned rubber gloves and delved into vile corners piling rubbish upon rubbish to be loaded into the skip, expecting at every moment to find a dead rat or a spider at least the size of a crab. Exuding resentment at the loss of each treasure, my husband hauled the stuff away, muttering sufficient incantations under his breath to turn me, at best, into a frog or a toad. Did he really think I was enjoying this?

Before long 'Oh, we don't need a skip, I'll take it to the tip' turned into 'You can't get much in you know. We could have done with a bigger skip'. By lunchtime the skip was indeed very full. And we were weary, filthy and hungry. We met in the kitchen and struggled to find the energy to pull open the fridge door. We need not have bothered. Milk and a pack of stale bacon were hardly going to make a meal. The phone rang. It was Rosemary, our friend from Thurlestone. 'You're supposed to be here for lunch!' she said. 'How long will you be?' We looked each other up and down, taking in the mould, the sawdust and the cobwebs thinking 'How long does it take to make a silk purse out of a sow's ear?' 20 minutes we agreed.

Suitably bathed and scrubbed we enjoyed a lunch that was delicious despite our late arrival. Our hostess was, as ever, charming and the other guests were kind and forgiving, remembering times when they too had forgotten to turn up to an event or arrived a day too early or a day too late. The thought of returning home to our chores became increasingly unappealing. But with the skip being collected the following day it was essential to keep going. So we changed back into our work clothes and cleared and swept until evening. The decorators would barely recognise their newly cleaned 'store room' when they returned. Thinking of decorators made my thoughts return to the wallpaper. And in particular the remaining scrap that had been laid for safety on top of a pile of dust sheets.

'Have you seen that piece of wallpaper?' I asked

'Which piece of wallpaper? I haven't seen any wallpaper.' Came the reply.

'The piece that was here, on top of those old dust sheets you threw away.'

'The dust sheets are in the skip.'

I looked around the neatly swept cellar, bare now except for paint pots and a pair of steps:

'Then the wallpaper must be in there too!'

And so in I had to go. Over the top. In amongst all the horrible old detritus and the imagined spiders and rats, poking about in the skip searching for that one precious piece of paper. Of course it was in the bottom, wet and muddy, beneath EVERYTHING. It tore in half as I pulled it. And then in half again as I pulled some more. The sound of a car approaching made me stand up as best I could. It was a rather nice Mercedes.

'Is that you Mrs. Dart?' asked the handsome young man who stepped from the car. I clasped my three bits of paper and considered hiding somewhere beneath the leaking radiator and a rusting mower, but there wasn't room. It is hard to assume any sort of dignity when only one's head and shoulders are visible above the deep metal sides and surrounding debris of a loaded skip. I imagined myself in the heat of battle, a tank commander with camouflage painted on my face.

'Yes.' I answered weakly.

'Have you lost something?' he asked.

I held up my stained scraps of paper:

'Oh dear!' Came the reply 'We are feeling hard up aren't we.'

He helped me gallantly as I jumped awkwardly from the skip.

'I've brought your chairs back, well five of them anyway.'

'Five?' I asked. 'What happened to the sixth?'

'Ah, well, the chair is all right. That's OK. Nothing to worry about there. It is just that, well, er, um, well, I've lost the piece of fabric I cut to cover it. And as you know, there isn't any more.'

'How do you mean, 'lost it'?

'Well I know I had it. But then it just seemed to disappear.'

Briefly, somewhere between wanting to scream or cry, I felt a sense of déjà vu and considered giving him Abigail's telephone number.

'Oh! Let's have a drink.' Stated my husband, sensing a touch of angst in the air 'I'll go and fetch a bottle.'

We sat in the kitchen on the hard garden chairs, not wanting to risk dirtying the pristine 5 and waited for him to return. After some time there was an anguished call for a pair of pliers.

'Pliers? Whatever for?'

'The decorators have removed the doorknob from the wine cellar and I can't get in!'

I don't suppose we will ever know if it was intended as punishment for delaying their progress, but the following day when I saw the decorators having to 'make good' our existing wallpaper with a sort of 'papier mache' of my salvaged scraps, I could not in all honesty have blamed them.